MY
ROSARY

MY ROSARY

Its Power and Mystery

A Book of Readings

Msgr. Charles Dollen

Illustrations by O. Scarpelli

ALBA · HOUSE   NEW · YORK

SOCIETY OF ST. PAUL, 2187 VICTORY BLVD., STATEN ISLAND, NEW YORK 10314

Library of Congress Cataloging-in-Publication Data

Dollen, Charles.
  My Rosary, its power and mystery.

  1. Rosary. 2. Catholic Church — Prayer-books and
devotions — English. I. Title.
BX2310.R7D65   1988   242'.74   87-33438
ISBN 0-8189-0529-8

_____

Designed, printed and bound in the United States of
America by the Fathers and Brothers of the
Society of St. Paul, 2187 Victory Boulevard,
Staten Island, New York 10314, as part of their
communications apostolate.

_____

1 2 3 4 5 6 7 8 9 (Current Printing: first digit)
_____

_____

DEDICATION

Edward and Beverly Kelly
and
David and Barbara Kelly

* * * * * * * ○ * * * * * * * ○ * * * * * * *

ACKNOWLEDGMENTS

Basic Bible readings from the New American Bible, St. Anthony Guild Edition. This text was chosen because of its liturgical usage (NAB).

Quotations from, or use of notes:
> The New Testament, Confraternity of Christian Doctrine. St. Anthony Guild Press (CCD).
> The New Testament, Msgr. Ronald Knox. Sheed & Ward (Knox).
> The New Jerusalem Bible, Doubleday (NJB).
> The Holy Bible, Revised Standard. Liturgical Press (RSV).

Excerpts were taken principally from my own previous books:
> *A Voice Said Ave!* St. Paul Editions.
> *Book of Catholic Wisdom.* Our Sunday Visitor Press.
> *Civil Rights: A Source Book.* St. Paul Editions.
> *Jesus, Lord.* St. Paul Editions.
> *Marmion: Fire of Love.* Herder.
> *Prayerbook of the Saints.* Our Sunday Visitor Press.
> *Prayers for the Third Age.* Our Sunday Visitor Press.
> *Ready or Not.* St. Paul Editions.
> *St. Augustine: The Trinity.* St. Paul Editions.
> *The Catholic Tradition* (14 v) Consortium Press.

Reference Works:
    Dictionary of the Bible. (John L. McKenzie) Bruce.
    Harper's Bible Dictionary. Harper & Row.
    Jerome Biblical Commentary. Prentice-Hall.
    Nelson's Concordance. The Liturgical Press.
    New Catholic Commentary. Nelson.
    New Catholic Encyclopedia. Catholic University.

Other excerpts are acknowledged from:
    Alphonsus Liguori, St. *The Glories of Mary.* Redemptorist.
    Callan, Charles. *The Acts of the Apostles.* Jos. F. Wagner.
    Carlen, Claudia. *The Papal Encyclicals, 1740-1981.* Consortium.
    Carretto, Carlo. *Blessed Are You Who Believed.* Orbis.
    Escriva, Josemaria. *The Way of the Cross.* Scepter.
    Farrell, Walter. *A Companion to the Summa.* Sheed & Ward.
    Goodier, Alban. *The Passion and Death of Our Lord Jesus Christ.* P.J. Kenedy.
    Grech, Prospero. *Acts of the Apostles Explained.* Alba House.
    Leon-Dufour, Xavier. *Resurrection and the Message of Easter.* Holt, Rinehart.
    Marmion, Columba. *Christ in His Mysteries.* Herder. *Christ the Life of the Soul.* Herder.
    O'Carroll, Michael. *Theotokos.* Michael Glazier.
    Perkins, Pheme. *Resurrection.* Doubleday.
    Perrin, Joseph-Marie. *Mary: Mother of Christ and of Christians.* Alba House.
    Riga, Peter. *The Redeeming Christ.* Corpus.
    Sabourin, Leopold. *Christology: Basic Texts in Focus.* Alba House.
    Sheed, Frank. *To Know Christ Jesus.* Sheed & Ward. *What Difference Does Jesus Make?* Sheed & Ward.
    Sheen, Fulton. *The Life of Christ.* Popular Library.

* * * * * * *   o   * * * * * * *   o   * * * * * * *

CONTENTS

INTRODUCTION

Pope Leo XIII: *Octobri Mense* (Sept. 22, 1891).

7. To appease the might of an outraged God and to bring that health of soul so needed by those who are sorely afflicted, there is nothing better than devout and persevering prayer, provided it be joined with a love and practice of Christian life. And both of these, the spirit of prayer and the practice of Christian life, are best attained through the devotion of the Rosary of Mary.

14. To this commendation of the Rosary which follows from the very nature of the prayer, We may add that the Rosary offers an easy way to present the chief mysteries of the Christian religion and to impress them upon the mind; and this commendation is one of the most beautiful of all.

For it is mainly by faith that one sets out on the straight and sure path to God and learns to revere in mind and heart His supreme majesty, His sovereignty over the whole creation, His unbounded power, wisdom and providence.

16. The Church has been in the habit of looking for the strongest support of faith in the Rosary of Mary. In the Rosary, along with the most beautiful and efficacious prayer arranged in an orderly fashion, the chief mysteries of our religion follow one another as they are brought before our mind for contemplation.

Pope Pius XI: *Ingravescentibus malis* (Sept. 29, 1937).

9. Among the various supplications with which we successfully appeal to the Virgin Mother of God, the Holy Rosary without doubt occupies a special and distinct place. This prayer, which some call the *Psalter of the Virgin* or *Breviary of the Gospel and of Christian Life* was described and recommended by Pope Leo XIII.

10. [Its usefulness] can well be deduced from the very flowers that form this mystic garland. What prayers in fact can be found more adaptable and holy?

This first is that which our Divine Redeemer Himself pronounced when His disciples asked Him, "Lord, teach us to pray" (Luke 11:1). . . . The other prayer is the Angelic Salutation which begins with the eulogies of the Archangel Gabriel and of St. Elizabeth, and ends with the very pious supplication by which we beg the help of the Blessed Virgin now, and at the hour of our death.

Pope Paul VI: *Christi Matri* (Sept. 15, 1966).

9. We want you to take the lead in urging and encouraging people to pray ardently to our most merciful mother Mary by saying the Rosary during the month of October. This prayer is well-suited to the People of God, most pleasing to the Mother of God and most effective in gaining heaven's blessings.

The Vatican Council recommended use of the Rosary to all in the Church, not in express words, but in unmistakable fashion in this phrase: "Let them highly value the pious practices and exercises directed to the Blessed Virgin and approved over the centuries by the magisterium."

*   *   *   *   *   *   *

The origin of the Rosary as we have it, the fifteen decades and the regular joyful, sorrowful and glorious mysteries, can be traced back historically to the Dominican, Blessed Alan de la Roche (c. 1425-1475). He piously referred it back to the founder of his order, St. Dominic, but that has only a vague and tenuous claim.

There were various forms of prayers in honor of the Blessed Virgin that were popular, and St. Dominic certainly promoted devotion to her. But at least in its "modern" form, if five centuries counts as that, it has been a most popular and efficacious devotion among Christian people.

The power of the Rosary consists in the various Christian mysteries that we meditate upon while we repeat familiar prayers. Certainly the mere repetition of prayers is not useful in itself, and Our Lord warned against that type of prayer. The fifteen mysteries form a powerful emphasis on the heart of Christianity which we impress upon ourselves in this prayer.

This study of these mysteries, plus some suggested alternatives, is meant to help clergy, religious and laity form an even more educated understanding of the power and the mysteries of the Most Holy Rosary.

The procedure will be to look at pertinent scriptural passages for each mystery, then to see how the more ancient writers viewed them, especially the Fathers of the Church, and then to present a few more recent authors on the subjects. Each chapter will conclude with my own personal meditation on the subject.

I have allowed myself a great deal of latitude on the amount of material included in each chapter and in each of the four sections of each chapter. This has been dictated mostly by the amount of material I found useful and helpful in each section.

The alternative mysteries have also been dictated by my own interests, and they are meant just to be typical of how mysteries can be expanded for special occasions and devotional needs. These are really indications of how the Rosary can be extended for spiritual profit and variety. They are generally kept rather brief.

PART ONE

THE JOYFUL MYSTERIES

* * * * * o * * * * * * * o * * * * *

I.
First Joyful Mystery:
THE ANNUNCIATION

1. SCRIPTURE

In the sixth month, the angel Gabriel was sent from God to a town of Galilee named Nazareth, to a virgin betrothed to a man named Joseph, of the house of David. The virgin's name was Mary.

Upon arriving, the angel said to her, "Rejoice, O highly favored daughter! The Lord is with you. Blessed are you among women." She was deeply troubled by his words and wondered what his greeting meant.

The angel went on to say to her: "Do not fear, Mary. You have found favor with God. You shall conceive and bear a son and give him the name Jesus. Great will be his dignity and he will be called Son of the Most High. The Lord God will give him the throne of David his father. He will rule over the house of Jacob forever and his reign will be without end."

Mary said to the angel, "How can this be since I do not know man?" The angel answered her: "The Holy Spirit will come upon you and the power of the Most High will overshadow you; hence, the holy offspring to be born will be called Son of God. Know that Elizabeth, your kinswoman has conceived a son in her old age; she who was thought to be sterile is now in her sixth month, for nothing is impossible with God."

Mary said: "I am the servant of the Lord. Let it be done to me as you say." With that the angel left her.

Luke 1:26-31   (NAB)

And he [the angel] came to her and said, "Hail, full of grace, the Lord is with you!"   Luke 1:28   (RSV)

And when the angel had come to her he said, "Hail, full of grace, the Lord is with thee. Blessed art thou among women."   Luke 1:28   (CCD)

Into her presence the angel came, and said, "Hail thou who art full of grace; the Lord is with thee; blessed art thou among women."   Luke 1:28   (Knox)

. . . Suddenly the angel of the Lord appeared in a dream and said to him: "Joseph, son of David have no fear about taking Mary as your wife. It is by the Holy Spirit that she has conceived this child. She is to have a son and you are to name him Jesus because he will save his people from their sins."

All this happened to fulfill what the Lord had said through the prophet: "The virgin shall be with child and give birth to a son, and they shall call him Emmanuel," a name which means "God is with us."

Matthew 1:20-23   (NAB)

Therefore the Lord himself will give you this sign: the virgin shall be with child and bear a son and shall name him Emmanuel.   Isaiah 7:14   (NAB)

His dominion is vast and forever peaceful, from David's throne, and over his kingdom, which he confirms and sustains by judgment and justice, both now and forever.

Isaiah 9:6   (NAB)

Then he brought me back to the outer gate of the sanctuary facing the east; but it was closed. He said to me: "This gate is to remain closed; it is not to be opened for anyone to enter by it; since the Lord, the God of Israel, has entered by it, it shall remain closed."

Ezekiel 44:1-2   (NAB)

[The Lord is speaking to Nathan about King David] "And when your time comes and you rest with your ancestors, I will raise up your heir after you, sprung from your loins, and I will make his kingdom firm. It is he who shall build a house for my name.

"And I will make his royal throne firm forever. I will be a father to him and he shall be a son to me. And, if he does wrong, I will correct him with the rod of men and with human chastisements; but I will not withdraw my favor from him as I withdrew it from your predecessor Saul, whom I removed from my presence.

"Your house and your kingdom shall endure forever before me; your throne shall stand firm forever."

2 Samuel 7:12-16   (NAB)

In the lifetime of those kings the God of heaven will set up a kingdom that shall never be destroyed or delivered up to another people; rather it shall break in pieces all these kingdoms and put an end to them, and it shall stand forever.   Daniel 2:44   (NAB)

Then this word of the Lord came to Jeremiah: "I am the Lord, the God of all mankind! Is anything impossible to me?"   Jeremiah 32:26-27   (NAB)

2. ANCIENT AUTHORS

St. Bernard: *Second Homily on the Missus Est*

"And the Virgin's name was Mary." Let us say a few things about this name, which can be interpreted as "Star of the Sea," an apt designation for the Mother of God.

She is most beautifully likened to a star, for a star pours forth its light without losing anything of its nature. She gave us her Son without losing anything of her virginity. The glowing rays of a star take nothing away from its beauty. Neither has the Son taken anything away from His Mother's integrity.

She is that noble star of Jacob, illuminating the whole world, penetrating from the highest heavens to the deepest depths of hell. The warmth of her brilliance shines in our minds, encouraging virtue, extinguishing vice. She is that glorious star lighting the way across this vast ocean of life, glowing with merits, guiding by example.

When you find yourself tossed by the raging storms on this great sea of life, far from land, keep your eyes fixed on this star to avoid disaster. When the winds of temptation or the rocks of tribulation threaten, look up to the star, call upon Mary!

When the waves of pride or ambition sweep over you, when the tide of detraction or jealousy runs against you, look up to the star, call upon Mary! When the shipwreck of avarice, anger or lust seems imminent, call upon Mary!

If the horror of sin overwhelms you and the voice of conscience terrifies you, if the fear of judgment, the abyss of sadness, and the depths of despair clutch at your heart, think of Mary! In dangers, difficulties and doubts, think of Mary, call upon Mary!

Keep her name on your lips, her love in your heart. Imitate her and her powerful intercession will surround you. Following her you will not stray. Praying to her you will ward off disaster and despair. Meditate about her and you will not err. Cling to her and you cannot fall.

With her protection, there is nothing to fear. Under her leadership, you will succeed. With her encouragement, all is possible.

And someday, you, yourself, will experience the depth of meaning in St. Luke's phrase, "And the Virgin's name was Mary." With only these few phrases of meditation, we are strengthened in the clarity of her brilliance. How much greater strength we can derive from them through silent contemplation!

In the scintillating light of this star our fervent service of her Son will glow ever more brilliant.

St. Sophronius: *On the Annunciation*

What does that blessed spirit, Gabriel, say when he is sent to a virgin so perfectly endowed with integrity? How does he present this, the happiest message of all time? "Hail, full of grace, the Lord is with you."

Joyfully he brings her the message of joy. How well he realized that this is an announcement of joy for all people, for all creatures, that it will mean the end of sorrow for all. He knows that the world will glow with the radiance of this divine mystery.

Rejoice, O Mother of sublime joy. Rejoice, O Mother of immortal joy. Rejoice, O God-bearing treasure-house of eternal joy, ever-flourishing tree of life-giving joy. Virgin before and after childbirth, rejoice! Mother of God, wonder of wonders, rejoice!

You have adorned human nature and been exalted

above all the orders of angels. You have been raised above every creature. Only you have been chosen to bear the Creator of all creatures in your womb, given Him to the world, pressed Him to your bosom.

Only you, from among all creatures, have been made the Mother of God.

St. Jerome: *Commentary on Ezekiel*

This gate shall be closed, says the prophet, and it will not be opened. Beautiful, indeed, is that closed gate through which only the Lord God of Israel may enter, the Leader for whom it has been closed.

The Blessed Virgin is that beautiful, closed gate. She was a virgin before childbirth, and she remained a virgin after childbirth. To the Virgin an angel said, "The Holy Spirit shall come over you and the power of the Most High God shall overshadow you; the Holy One to be born of you will be called the Son of God." She remained a virgin after He was born. Forever, Mary is a virgin.

Some have falsely claimed that the "brethren of the Lord" mentioned in Scripture are children born to Mary from Joseph. This is definitely wrong to say about the ever-virgin Mary, who is the closed gate that will not be opened.

3. RECENT AUTHORS

Bishop John Lancaster Spalding: *Ave Maria Bells*, v.1

> At dawn the joyful choir of bells,
> In consecrated citadels.
> Flings on the sweet and drowsy air,
> A brief, melodious call to prayer;
> For Mary, Virgin meek and lowly
> Conceived of the Spirit Holy,
> As the Lord's angel did declare.

Hilaire Belloc: *Courtesy*, vv.1-3

Of courtesy, it is much less
Than courage of heart or holiness,
Yet in my walk it seems to me
That the grace of God is in courtesy.

On monks I did in Storrington fall,
They took me straight into their hall;
I saw three pictures on a wall,
And courtesy was in them all.

The first the Annunciation;
The second the Visitation;
The third the Consolation
Of God that was Our Lady's Son.

Father G. Graystone, S.M.: "The Mother of Jesus in the Scriptures" in *A New Catholic Commentary on Holy Scripture*

In the striking introduction (Lk 1:26) Mary is presented as a virgin, a word applied to no other woman in the New Testament as a title, and as a 'virgin betrothed'. The note of paradox is accentuated by Mary's subsequent question, 'How shall this be since I know not man?' (v.34). The traditional explanation, that Mary had already resolved (possibly vowed) perpetual virginity, still seems the most natural, both in the immediate context and in the wider literary and theological setting of Luke 1-2.

The Angel greets Mary with a salutation never before heard in Scripture. 'Hail' is better rendered 'rejoice', the etymological meaning. In the light of what follows, it alludes to the prophetical oracles addressed to the Daughter of Zion (Israel personified), bidding her rejoice and fear not because the Lord, her King, is in the midst of her as Savior.

'Daughter of Zion' is now no longer a symbol, but a living reality. Mary sums up in herself the expectations of her people.

'Full of grace' according to the several senses of the Greek term, can be rendered 'highly favored' or 'favored one' or 'adorned with grace' or 'gracious, pleasing.' It should be noted that the form used denotes a lasting and permanent effect, and that it takes the place of a proper name. Mary is, *par excellence* God's Favorite, permanent object of his predilection, full of grace.

The Child to be born is announced in terms of the messianic title as Savior, King and Son of David.

4. MEDITATION

St. Gabriel, whose name means "the Strength of God," has himself been saluted through all the Christian centuries as a very special archangel, trusted by God for the message which would start off the whole action of the New Dispensation.

This mystery is so easy to dramatize in one's imagination. Where did the Annunciation take place, what form did Gabriel assume, was Mary at prayer at that time, who did she first tell about the vision? The Fathers of the Church, when they comment on this passage in Luke, all add their own details. It's a fascinating occupation that anyone can attempt.

Mary's Fiat is the key to the Incarnation. God asks her permission — and, the thought occurs, she could have said "No." What would have happened then? St. Bernard pictures all the choirs of angels in heaven and the entire cast of Old Testament characters collectively holding their breath while Mary ponders.

But of course, she wouldn't say "No." Mary was so in tune with the will of God, so perfectly and completely "full of grace," that, as soon as she knew what God wanted of her, she would agree. And when she did, "The Word became flesh and dwelt among us" (Jn 1:14).

There is ample food for thought in all of this, but one aspect that frequently appeals to me in this mystery, is the importance of seeking the will of God, and asking for the courage to follow it as perfectly as possible.

* * * * * * *   o   * * * * * * *   o   * * * * * * *

II.
Second Joyful Mystery:
THE VISITATION

1. SCRIPTURE

Thereupon, Mary set out, proceeding in haste into the hill country to a town of Judah, where she entered Zechariah's house and greeted Elizabeth. When Elizabeth heard Mary's greeting, the baby leapt in her womb.

Elizabeth was filled with the Holy Spirit and cried out in a loud voice: "Blest are you among women and blest is the fruit of your womb. But who am I that the mother of my Lord should come to me? The moment your greeting sounded in my ears, the baby leapt in my womb for joy. Blest is she who trusted that the Lord's words to her would be fulfilled."

Then Mary said:
> "My being proclaims the greatness of the Lord,
>   my spirit finds joy in God my savior,
> For he has looked upon his servant in her lowliness;
>   all ages to come shall call me blessed.
> God who is mighty has done great things for me,
>   holy is his name;
> His mercy is from age to age
>   on those who fear him,

17

He has shown might with his arm;
    he has confused the proud in their inmost
        thoughts.
He has deposed the mighty from their thrones
    and raised the lowly to high places.
The hungry he has given every good thing,
    while the rich he has sent empty away.
He has upheld Israel his servant,
    ever mindful of his mercy;
Even as he promised our fathers,
    promised Abraham and his descendants
        forever."

Mary remained with Elizabeth about three months and then returned home.   Luke 1:39-56   (NAB)

[The Canticle of Hannah, the mother of Samuel]

"My heart exults in the Lord,
    my horn is exalted in my God.
I have swallowed up my enemies;
    I rejoice in my victory.
There is no Holy One like the Lord;
    there is no Rock like our God.
Speak boastfully no longer,
    nor let arrogance issue from your mouths.
For an all-knowing God is the Lord,
    a God who judges deeds.
The bows of the mighty are broken,
    while the tottering gird on strength.
The well-fed hire themselves out for bread,
    while the hungry batten on spoil.
The barren wife bears seven sons,
    while the mother of many languishes.

The Lord puts to death and gives life;
    he cast down to the nether world;
        he raises up again.
The Lord makes poor and makes rich,
    he humbles, he also exalts.
He raises the needy from the dust;
    from the ash heap he lifts up the poor,
To seat them with nobles
    and make a glorious throne their heritage.
He gives to the vower his vow,
    and blesses the sleep of the just.
For the pillars of the earth are the Lord's,
    and he has set the world upon them.
He will guard the footsteps of his faithful ones,
    but the wicked shall perish in the darkness.
For not by strength does man prevail;
    the Lord's foes shall be shattered.
The Most High in heaven thunders;
    the Lord judges the ends of the earth.
Now may he give strength to his king,
    and exalt the horn of his anointed!"

                    1 Samuel 2:1-10   (NAB)

Then David, girt with a linen apron, came dancing before the Lord with abandon, as he and all the Israelites were bringing up the Ark of the Lord with shouts of joy and the sound of the horn. As the Ark of the Lord was entering the City of David, Saul's daughter Michal looked down through the window and saw King David leaping and dancing before the Lord and she despised him in her heart.

The Ark of the Lord was brought in and set in its place within the tent David had pitched for it. Then David offered holocausts and peace offerings before the Lord.

                    2 Samuel 6:14-17   (NAB)

And in your descendants all the nations of the earth shall find blessing — all this because you obeyed my command.
                                          Genesis 22:18   (NAB)

Blessed among women be Jael, blessed among tent-dwelling women.
                                          Judges 5:24   (NAB)

I rejoice heartily in the Lord,
    in my God is the joy of my soul;
For he has clothed me with a robe of salvation,
    and wrapped me in a mantle of justice,
Like a bridegroom adorned with a diadem,
    like a bride bedecked with her jewels.
                                          Isaiah 61:10   (NAB)

But God is the judge;
    one he brings low; another he lifts up.
                                          Psalm 75:8   (NAB)

He has remembered his kindness and his faithfulness
    toward the house of Israel.
All the ends of the earth have seen
    the salvation by our God.   Psalm 98:3   (NAB)

But the kindness of the Lord is from eternity
    to eternity toward those who fear him,
And his justice toward children's children
    among those who keep his covenant
    and remember to fulfill his precepts.
                                          Psalm 103:17-18   (NAB)

Because he satisfied the longing soul
    and filled the hungry soul with good things.
                                          Psalm 107:9   (NAB)

The Lord is exalted, yet the lowly he sees,
  and the proud he knows from afar.

                                   Psalm 138:6   (NAB)

2. ANCIENT AUTHORS

St. Basil: *Commentary on Isaiah*

I went into the prophetess, he says, and she conceived
and gave birth to a son. That Mary was the prophetess to
whom Isaiah drew near in spirit, is clear to those who remember Mary's words which she spoke under the influence
of a prophetic spirit.

Her words? "My soul magnifies the Lord, and my spirit
exults in God, my Savior, because He has taken notice of me,
His handmaiden. From now on, every generation shall call
me blessed."

If we listen carefully to these words, we cannot deny
that she was a prophetess. The Spirit of the Lord had come
upon her, and the power of the Most High God had overshadowed her.

St. Ambrose: *Homily on Luke*

It is clear to everyone that when faith is demanded, the
reason for believing must be shown. Therefore, when the
angel announced so mysterious a message to Mary, he immediately gave as a proof the news that the elderly, sterile
Elizabeth had conceived, "that you may realize that all
things are possible with God."

When Mary heard this, she hastened off to the mountain village, not because she was incredulous about the
prophecy, uncertain about the messenger, or doubtful
about the fact. She went to rejoice in the answer to prayer;

she was prepared to help in fraternal charity; she hastened
to participate in happiness.

When one is filled with God, it is natural to desire to
advance still further. Indeed, the Holy Spirit expects us to
make good use of grace.

We can learn to advance in virtue from the example of
Mary. See her solicitude for a relative who was with child.
Mary's modesty, which previously kept her from much contact with people, did not keep her from undertaking a
difficult journey when a work of charity was involved.

When the Virgin knew she was needed, she did not
think up excuses or plead the weakness of her sex. She left
home immediately and hastened into the mountain country
to be of service. . . .

Mary left home promptly when needed and even remained three months in her cousin's service. She visits simply as a cousin from some distance, as a junior to a senior.
Not only did this noble Virgin come, she was the first to offer
a greeting.

Meditate on this. The superior comes to the lesser one:
Mary to Elizabeth; Christ to John. Later Christ comes to
John at the River Jordan.

Notice how quickly benefits result from Mary's visit and
Christ's presence. Elizabeth first heard Mary's voice, but
John first sensed the nearness of grace. Elizabeth heard in
the natural order; John exulted in the mysterious order of
grace. Elizabeth acknowledges Mary; John responds to
Christ.

The two mothers speak words of grace; the two infants
communicate on the spiritual plane. As the mothers draw
close in fraternal charity, by a two-fold miracle, they prophesy in the spirit of their children.

The baby exults and the mother is filled with the Holy
Spirit. The son receives the Holy Spirit first, and only then

does his mother receive it. Then she cried out, "How wonderful it is that the Mother of my Lord comes to me!" That is, this is a great and unexpected honor that the Mother of the Lord, a woman so singularly chosen, should be coming here to see me. I sense a miracle. I acknowledge the mystery — the Mother of my Lord even now carries the Divine Word within Her.

St. Bernardine of Siena: *Sermon on the Visitation*

Among all the human race, who can even be thought of as purer than she who merited to become the Mother of God, who for nine months had God for her Guest in her heart and in her womb? What greater treasure is there than Divine Love Himself, burning in the heart of the Virgin, as in a furnace?

. . . The Mother and Mistress of Wisdom speaks few words, but each is filled with great depths of meaning. We read that the Mother of Christ spoke seven times, seven words filled with wisdom, as if to show, mystically, that she is filled with the sevenfold graces.

Twice she spoke to the angel and twice to Elizabeth. She also spoke to her Son twice, and once at the wedding feast, where she also spoke to the attendants.

On all these occasions, she spoke very little, except for the one time when the praises of God just poured forth from her lips in thanksgiving. Then she said, "My soul doth magnify the Lord." But note that here she is speaking to God, not to men.

3. RECENT AUTHORS

M.E. McIver: "The Visitation of Mary," in *The New Catholic Encyclopedia*

The use of Old Testament texts to communicate a deeper theological meaning is evident here. Mary, the Virgin Daughter of Zion, the dwelling place of Yahweh, and the perfect eschatological personification of Israel, is presented in the Visitation account.

There is a marked literary dependence on [1 Sam 2 for the Magnificat] and on 2 Samuel 6:9-15, which tells the story of the bringing of the Ark to Jerusalem by David. As David and his friends rejoiced in the presence of the Ark, so did Elizabeth and her unborn child in the presence of Mary.

As David leaped for joy before the Ark, so did John in his mother's womb. The cry of David, "How shall the Ark of the Lord come to me?" is echoed by that of Elizabeth, "How have I deserved that the mother of my Lord should come to me?"

Father Raymond E. Brown: *The Birth of the Messiah*

The poverty and hunger of the oppressed in the Magnificat are primarily spiritual, but we should not forget the physical realities faced by the early Christians. The first followers of Jesus were Galileans; and Galilee, victimized by the absentee ownership of estates, was the spawning ground of first century revolts against a repressive occupation and the taxation it engendered.

There was real poverty among the Jerusalem Christians who became the nucleus of the post-Resurrection Church. And when the gospel was proclaimed in the Diaspora among Jews and Gentiles, frequently it attracted the underprivileged social classes. . . .

And so vv 51-53 of the Magnificat would resonate among such groups; for them the Christian good news meant that the ultimately blessed were not the mighty and the rich who tyrannized them. Reformers of all times have advocated revolutions that would level class distinctions by making the poor sufficiently rich and the powerless sufficiently powerful.

But the Magnificat anticipates the Lucan Jesus in preaching that wealth and power are not real values since they have no standing in God's sight. This is not an easy message even for those who profess credence in Jesus.

By introducing it as a leit motiv in the hymns of the infancy narrative, Luke has begun to introduce the offense of the cross into the good news proclaimed by Gabriel. If for Luke Mary is the first Christian disciple, it is fitting that he place on her lips sentiments that Jesus will make the hallmark of the disciple in the main gospel story.

It is no accident, then, that some of the offense of the cross rubbed off on Mary. In the early dialogue between Christians and Jews one of the objections against Christianity is that God would never have had His Messiah come into the world without fitting honor and glory, born of a woman who admitted that she was no more than a handmaiden, a female slave.

4. MEDITATION

Mary goes with haste, or as some translate, with a thoughtful heart, to the hill-country town probably about six miles from Jerusalem. Luke tells us only of the greetings between the two prophetesses, and even that little bit is filled with the spirit of Old Testament spirituality.

What patriarchs, prophets, priests and kings had longed for for so many centuries was now coming into human history. What they had heard preached and discussed every Sabbath in the synagogues was now about to happen. What they had prayed over in psalms and canticles they would not simply witness — they would be an integral part of it.

There was a fullness here over which they exulted. How their hearts and minds and words must have sung with joy and with the praises of God. It really staggers the imagination.

Mary's words in the Magnificat are a true canticle to God, witnessing to the promises fulfilled to Abraham, Jacob, Moses and David. They were also a prophecy of what the messianic age would inaugurate.

In this mystery we are invited to join as disciples with two of the first Christian believers.

* * * * * * *   ○   * * * * * * *   ○   * * * * * * *

III.
Third Joyful Mystery
THE NATIVITY

1. SCRIPTURE

This is how the birth of Jesus Christ came about. When his mother Mary was engaged to Joseph, but before they lived together, she was found with child through the power of the Holy Spirit. Joseph, her husband, an upright man unwilling to expose her to the law, decided to divorce her quietly.

Such was his intention when suddenly the angel of the Lord appeared to him in a dream and said to him: "Joseph, son of David, have no fear about taking Mary as your wife. It is by the Holy Spirit that she has conceived this child. She is to have a son and you are to name him Jesus because he will save his people from their sins."

All this happened to fulfill what the Lord had said through the prophet [Isaiah 7:14]:

> "The virgin shall be with child
> and give birth to a son,
> and they shall call him Emmanuel"

29

a name which means "God is with us." When Joseph awoke he did as the angel of the Lord had directed him and received her into his home as his wife. He had no relations with her at any time before she bore a son, whom he named Jesus.   Matthew 1:18-25   (NAB)

In those days Caesar Augustus published a decree ordering a census of the whole world. This first census took place while Quirinius was governor of Syria. Everyone went to register, each to his own town.

And so Joseph went from the town of Nazareth in Galilee to Judea, to David's town of Bethlehem — because he was of the house and lineage of David — to register with Mary, his espoused wife, who was with child.

While they were there the days of her confinement were completed. She gave birth to her first-born son and wrapped him in swaddling clothes and laid him in a manger, because there was no room for them in the place where travelers lodged.

There were shepherds in that locality, living in the fields and keeping night watch by turns over their flocks. The angel of the Lord appeared to them as the glory of the Lord shone around them, and they were very much afraid.

The angel said to them: "You have nothing to fear! I come to proclaim good news to you — tidings of great joy to be shared by the whole people. This day in David's city a savior has been born to you, the Messiah and Lord. Let this be a sign to you: in a manger you will find an infant wrapped in swaddling clothes."

Suddenly, there was with the angel a multitude of the heavenly host, praising God and saying:

"Glory to God in high heaven,
Peace on earth to those on whom his favors rests."

When the angels had returned to heaven, the shepherds said to one another, "Let us go over to Bethlehem and see this event which the Lord has made known to us." They went in haste and found Mary and Joseph, and the baby lying in the manger; once they saw, they understood what had been told them concerning this child. All who heard of it were astonished at the report given them by the shepherds.

Mary treasured all these things and reflected on them in her heart. The shepherds returned, glorifying and praising God for all they had heard and seen, in accord with what had been told them.   Luke 2:1-20   (NAB)

And she brought forth her firstborn son, and wrapped him in swaddling clothes and laid him in a manger, because there was no room for them in the inn.   Luke 2:7   (CCD)

And she gave birth to her first-born son and wrapped him in swaddling cloths, and laid him in a manger, because there was no place for them in the inn.   Luke 2:7   (RSV)

In the beginning was the Word;
the Word was in God's presence,
and the Word was God.
He was present to God in the beginning.
Through him all things came into being,
and apart from him nothing came to be.
Whatever came to be in him found life,
life for the light of men.
The light shines on in darkness,
a darkness that did not overcome it. . . .
He was in the world,
and through him the world was made,
yet the world did not know who he was.

To his own he came,
yet his own did not accept him.
Any who did accept him
he empowered to become children of God.
These are they who believe in his name — who were
begotten not by blood, nor by carnal desire, nor by
man's willing it, but by God.
The Word became flesh
and made his dwelling among us,
and we have seen his glory;
The glory of an only Son coming from the Father,
filled with enduring love.   John 1:10-14   (NAB)

2. ANCIENT AUTHORS

St. Justin Martyr: *The First Apology*

For by God's power He was conceived by a Virgin who
was a descendant of Jacob, who was the father of Judah, the
father of the Jewish race; and Jesse was His forefather
according to the prophecy of Isaiah, and He was the son of
Jacob and Judah according to his lineage.

And again, hear how it was expressly foretold by Isaiah
that He was to be born of a Virgin. Here is the prophecy:
"Behold a Virgin shall conceive and bear a son and His name
shall be called Emmanuel" (i.e. God with us). For, what man
has deemed incredible and impossible, God foretold
through prophetic spirit as about to take place — so that,
when they took place, they should not be denied but believed, because they had been foretold.

Let us attempt to explain the words of the prophecy.
The words, "Behold a virgin shall conceive" therefore mean
that the Virgin shall conceive without intercourse. For if she

had intercourse with anyone whomever, she was no longer a virgin, but the power of God descending upon the Virgin overshadowed her and caused her, while still a virgin, to conceive.

St. Leo: *7th Sermon on the Nativity*

The man who rejoices in today's feast is a man of true devotion and reverence, with no false notions of the Incarnation of the Lord or of the deity. It would be equally false to deny that Christ has a truly human nature, like ours, as it would be to deny that He is equal in glory to the Father.

When we attempt to understand the mystery of the Nativity of Christ, Who was born of a Virgin Mother, the mists of earthly reason must be banished and the smoke of mundane wisdom must be swept from eyes illuminated by faith.

We believe on divine authority. We follow a divine doctrine. Whether we are moved to believe the testimony of the Law, the words of the Prophet, or the message of the Gospel, John, guided by the Holy Spirit, enunciates the great truth:

"In the beginning was the Word, and the Word was with God, and the Word was God. He was with God from the very beginning. All creatures were made by Him, and without Him nothing was created."

And the same teacher continues with another great truth: "The Word was made flesh and dwelled with us. We have seen His glory, the glory of the only-begotten of the Father."

In both natures, then, it is the same Son of God. He takes our nature but loses nothing that is proper to Himself. He shares our manhood to renew man, but He remains unchangeable in Himself. The Divine Nature that He has in common with His Father suffers no loss of omnipotence, nor does the form of the servant violate the form of God.

The supreme and eternal essence which bowed down to man's low estate for our salvation and which, indeed, takes us up into His love, remained what it was. So, whenever the only begotten Son of God calls Himself less than the Father, of Whom He also says He is His equal, He acknowledges the truth of having both natures in Himself. The inequality proves Him human; the equality proves Him divine.

St. Augustine: *Against the Errors of Faustus*

He took the form of a servant in the womb of the Virgin, even though He has the nature of God. Equal to the Father, He did not think it wrong to claim that equality.

St. Paul makes the same declaration elsewhere openly: "When the fullness of time came, God sent His Son, born of a woman, born under the Law, to redeem those subject to the Law, that we might receive the adoption of sons."

(Galatians 4:4-5)

Jesus Christ is the Son of God and the Lord of David because of His divinity. He is the Son of David from the seed of David, according to His humanity. If this were not so vital to us, St. Paul would not have insisted to Timothy, "Remember this. According to my gospel, Jesus Christ, of the seed of David, has risen from the dead."   (2 Timothy 2:8)

It should certainly bother no follower of the holy Gospels that Jesus Christ, who was born of the Virgin without any intimacies with St. Joseph, is called the Son of David. Matthew the Evangelist traces the lineage of Christ not down to Mary, but to Joseph.

One and the same narrator tells approvingly that Joseph is the husband of Mary, that the Mother of Christ is a

Virgin, that Christ is of the seed of David, and that Joseph is in the line of Christ's progenitors from David.

St. Bernard: *On the Circumcision*

Yet, see how this Mediator between God and man, from the very instant of His birth joins the divine and the human, the highest and the lowest. He is born of a woman, but in such a way that the flower of her virginity is not harmed in any way by her motherhood.

He is wrapped in swaddling clothes, but even in this humble garb He is praised by angelic choirs. He is tucked away in a manger but a radiant star keeps watch.

3. RECENT AUTHORS

Prosper Gueranger: *The Liturgical Year*

With regard to our Savior's birth on December 25, we have St. John Chrysostom telling us, in his homily for this feast, that the Western Churches had, from the very commencement of Christianity, kept it on this day. He is not satisfied with merely mentioning the tradition; he undertakes to show that it is well-founded, inasmuch as the Church of Rome had every means of knowing the true day of our Savior's birth since the acts of enrollment, taken in Judea, were kept in the public archives of Rome.

The holy doctor adds a second argument which he founds on the Gospel of St. Luke, and he reasons thus: we know from the Sacred Scripture that it must have been in the fast in the seventh month that the priest Zachary had the vision in the Temple; after which Elizabeth his wife conceived St. John the Baptizer; hence it follows that the

Blessed Virgin Mary having, as the evangelist St. Luke relates, received the angel Gabriel's visit and conceived the
Savior of the world in the sixth month of Elizabeth's preg-
nancy, that is to say, in March, the birth of Jesus must have
taken place in the month of December.

Karl Adam: *The Spirit of Catholicism*

The Incarnation is for Christians the foundation and
the planting of that new communion which we call the
Church. The Body of Christ and the Kingdom of God came
into being as objective reality at the moment when the Word
was made Flesh.

In her, the divine is objectivized, is incarnated in the
community, and precisely and only in so far as it is a
community.

Carlo Carretto: *Blessed Are You Who Believed*

So now I am no longer frightened. If God is that baby
lying on the straw in the cave, God cannot frighten me.

I can be afraid of my father, yes, especially if I don't
really know him; but of my son, never.

Of my son whom I hold in my arms, whom I cradle at
my breast; of my son who asks me for protection and
warmth, oh no.

I cannot be afraid.

I cannot be afraid.

I cannot be afraid any more. Peace, which is the absence
of fear, now abides in me.

Now the only task that remains to me is to believe.

And believing is like generating. In faith I continue to
generate Jesus as son.

(This is what Mary did. It was easy enough for her to
generate Jesus in the flesh; nine months were enough.

But to generate, give birth to, Jesus in faith — for that she needed her whole life from Bethlehem to Calvary.)

Mary, like you I believe that this baby is both God and your son and I adore him.

I adore him in the pyx I am wearing under my cloak where he is hidden beneath the very frail sign of bread, frailer even than flesh.

I hear you, Mary, repeating every now and then, as at Bethlehem: "My God, my son. My God, my son."

4. MEDITATION

Christian ingenuity and love delights in finding ways to express the message of Christmas. It may be the stark retelling of the simple facts by St. Matthew and St. Luke or the brilliant expressions of faith by saints like St. Leo the Great and St. Bernard. It may be the theological brilliance of a Karl Adam or the dramatic meditation of a Carlo Carretto, but each age has delighted in retelling the story and adding its own distinctive and devotional application.

Masterpieces by artists and the works of poets and musicians continually try to add their tribute to the Christ-Child. The Emmanuel of Isaiah has become, for us, the Incarnate Son of God, a living force in history, a real presence in the Eucharist and in His Church.

But for all that 2000 years have produced, this mystery still beckons us forward. And another 2000 years will not exhaust the mystery. The central characters — Jesus, Mary and Joseph, and the supporting cast of Angels, shepherds and, a little later, the Magi — will continue to exercise their fascination.

Even that anonymous innkeeper who "had no place for them in the inn," will be the starting point for many a sermon. And the neighbors? Like women of all ages and places, they must have come to help this young mother with her first-born.

The world which could not destroy the fact of Christmas with persecution, hatred or indifference, now threatens it with an unparalleled celebration of the material. They would overwhelm Christmas with the frenzy of buying and selling of gifts, and then turning off the Christmas carols as soon as the cash register bells stop ringing.

In the Rosary, we let the spirit of Christmas grow deeper and deeper in our consciousness every time we pray this mystery.

IV.

Fourth Joyful Mystery
THE PRESENTATION

1. SCRIPTURE

When the day came to purify them according to the law of Moses, the couple brought him up to Jerusalem so that he could be presented to the Lord, for it is written in the law of the Lord, "Every first-born male shall be consecrated to the Lord." They came to offer in sacrifice "a pair of turtledoves or two young pigeons," in accord with the dictate in the law of the Lord.

There lived in Jerusalem at the time a certain man named Simeon. He was just and pious, and awaited the consolation of Israel, and the Holy Spirit was upon him. It was revealed to him by the Holy Spirit that he would not experience death until he had seen the Anointed of the Lord. He came to the temple now, inspired by the Spirit; and when the parents brought in the child Jesus to perform for him the customary ritual of the law, he took him in his arms and blessed God in these words:

> "Now, Master, you can dismiss your servant
>   in peace:
>   you have fulfilled your word.
> For my eyes have witnessed your saving deed
>   displayed for all the peoples to see:
> A revealing light to the Gentiles,
>   the glory of your people Israel."

The child's father and mother were marveling at what was being said about him. Simeon blessed them and said to Mary his mother: "This child is destined to be the downfall and the rise of many in Israel, a sign that will be opposed — and you yourself shall be pierced with a sword — so that the thoughts of many hearts may be laid bare."

There was also a certain prophetess, Anna by name, daughter of Phanuel of the tribe of Asher. She had seen many days, having lived seven years with her husband after her marriage, and then as a widow until she was eighty-four. She was constantly in the temple, worshipping day and night in fasting and prayer. Coming on the scene at this moment, she gave thanks to God and talked about the child to all who looked forward to the deliverance of Jerusalem.

When the pair had fulfilled all the prescriptions of the law of the Lord, they returned to Galilee and their own town of Nazareth. The child grew in size and strength, filled with wisdom, and the grace of God was upon him.

Luke 2:22-40 (NAB)

The Lord said to Moses, "Tell the Israelites: When a woman has conceived and gives birth to a boy, she shall be unclean for seven days, with the same uncleanness as at her menstrual period. On the eighth day, the flesh of the boy's foreskin shall be circumcised, and then she shall spend thirty-three days more in becoming purified of her blood;

she shall not touch anything sacred nor enter the sanctuary till the days of her purification are fulfilled.

"When the days of her purification . . . are fulfilled, she shall bring to the priest at the entrance of the meeting tent a yearling lamb for a holocaust and a pigeon or a turtledove for a sin offering. The priest shall offer them up before the Lord to make atonement for her, and thus she will be clean again after her flow of blood. . . . If, however, she cannot afford a lamb, she may take two turtledoves or two pigeons, the one for a holocaust and the other for a sin offering. The priest shall make atonement for her, and thus she will again be clean."   Leviticus 12:1-8   (NAB)

The Lord spoke to Moses and said, "Consecrate to me every first-born that opens the womb among the Israelites, both of man and beast, for it belongs to me."
                              Exodus 13:1-2   (NAB)

I am bringing on my justice, it is not far off,
    my salvation shall not tarry;
I will put salvation within Zion,
    and give to Israel my glory.
                              Isaiah 46:13   (NAB)
It is too little, he says, for you to be my servant,
    to raise up the tribes of Jacob,
    and restore the survivors of Israel;
I will make you a light to the nations,
    that my salvation may reach to the ends
        of the earth.
                              Isaiah 49:6   (NAB)
The Lord has bared his holy arm
    in the sight of all the nations;
All the ends of the earth will behold
    the salvation of our God.   Isaiah 52:10   (NAB)

Jesus spoke to them once again: "I am the light of the world. No follower of mine shall ever walk in darkness; no, he shall possess the light of life."   John 8:12   (NAB)

2. ANCIENT AUTHORS

St. Augustine: *13th Sermon for the Season*

Once it was foretold, "the Mother of Sion says, 'A Man shall be made in her and the Most High God, Himself, shall establish her.' " O Omnipotence being born! O magnificence of heaven descending to earth!

While still being carried in the womb, He is saluted by John the Baptizer, still in his mother's womb. Presented in the Temple, He is acknowledged by Simeon, an old man who was well-known, aged, proved, crowned. Simeon first recognized Him, then adored Him, and then exclaimed, "Now dismiss your servant in peace, O Lord, for I have seen your gift of salvation, personally."

Simeon's exit from the world was delayed so that he might see Him born Who had founded the world. The ancient one knew the Infant; in this Child he became a child again. Filled as he was with faith, he was renewed in his old age.

Simeon, the old man, carries the Infant Christ; Christ the Infant rules the old man, Simeon. He had been told by the Lord that he would not taste death until he had seen Christ the Lord, born. Christ was born, and the desire, so old in this man's yearning, is fulfilled in his old age. He Who found a world growing old comes to an old man.

Simeon did not desire to stay long in this world. He desired to see Christ come into the world chanting with the prophet the words, "Show us your mercy, O Lord, and grant us your salvation." And finally, that it may be evident that this happiness is full, he concludes with, "Now dismiss your servant in peace, for I have seen your gift of salvation personally."

The prophets joyfully foretold that the Creator of heaven and earth would some day be on earth with man. The angel announced that the Creator of body and soul would come in His own body. John, from the womb, saluted the Savior in Mary's womb. Simeon, the old man, acknowledged God, the Infant.

St. Ambrose: *Second Book of Commentaries on Luke*

And there was a just man in Jerusalem, named Simeon, devoutly awaiting the consolation of Israel. Testimony to the birth of the Lord is given not only by angels, prophets and shepherds, but also by just men and elders. All ages and both sexes, as well as miraculous events, strengthen our faith.

A Virgin conceives and a sterile woman is found with child. Elizabeth prophesies and her mute husband speaks. The Magi adore and a closed womb sends an exultant greeting. A widow acknowledges and a just man recognizes.

[Simeon] is well called a just man who does not seek his own, but rather his people's consolation. For himself, he desires that the chains that bind him to the flesh be dissolved, yet, while waiting, he longs to see the promise fulfilled. He knows how blessed are the eyes that will see Him.

He received Him in his embrace and, blessing God, he said, "Now dismiss your servant in peace, O Lord, according to your word." See, here, a just man imprisoned in the body, but desiring to be released that he may be with Christ. He knows that it is a great favor to be released from this life in order to be with Christ.

Let anyone who wishes to share this favor come to the Temple, come to Jerusalem, await Christ the Lord, receive the Word of God in his arms and embrace Him by good works, as the strong arms of faith. Then he, too, will be dismissed, not that he will never see death, but because he has seen Life.

See how grace has been poured out copiously at the birth of Our Lord. Prophecy is given to just men, withheld from the unbelieving. Simeon foretells that the Lord Jesus Christ has come for the raising up, or the ruin, of many men, and that the merits of the just and of the wicked will be thoroughly scrutinized. According to the quality of our works, this Judge, just and true, will decide.

St. Bernard: *Commentary on the Twelve Stars*

The martyrdom of the Virgin, begun in the prophecy of Simeon, reaches its height in the history of the passion of Our Lord. To the Infant Jesus Simeon had said, "This Child is to be a sign which will be contradicted." To the Mother he had said, "A sword will pierce your very soul!"

O truly Blessed Mother, the sword has pierced. The only way it could cut was to see the piercing of your Divine Son. After He has breathed His last, when the cruel sword could not touch His Spirit as it passed through His side, surely it pierced your own soul.

His soul was no longer there, but yours did not draw back. Surely it received the wound. We call you more than a martyr because the passion of sense pain was exceeded by the compassion of love.

He died because His love is greater than any man's; she died because there is no love like hers among men. This is indeed the twelfth prerogative, the twelfth star in her crown — her martyrdom of heart.

3. RECENT AUTHORS

Father James Alberione, S.S.P.: *Mary, Hope of the World*

When forty days had passed, Mary went to the Temple for the double ceremony of purification and presentation. What an example of humility! (Lk 2:22-24)

The Virgin Mother fulfilled the offering of her Son. The offering was accepted and consummated on Calvary.

A venerable old man, Simeon by name, just and devout, was awaiting the consolation of Israel. The Holy Spirit was in him and had revealed to him that he would not die before seeing the Christ of the Lord. Led by the Holy Spirit, he went to the Temple. Yielding to his desires, Mary placed the Divine Infant in his arms. Simeon took Him, contemplated Him with ardent love, and enthusiastically exclaimed, "Now Master you can dismiss your servant in peace. . . ." (Lk 2:29-32)

Mary and Joseph were greatly impressed; how did Simeon know the secret of the Messiah? Suddenly, however, the old man interrupted his blessing and his face grew troubled. He turned to the young Mother and said: "This child is destined to be the downfall and the rise of many in Israel . . . and you yourself will be pierced with a sword. . . ." (Lk 2:34-35)

What an impression these words must have made on Mary's soul! From that moment on, always before her eyes was a vision of persecution, calumny, anxieties, agony and death.

The elderly prophetess Anna, daughter of Phanuel, of the tribe of Asher, was also present at this scene, for she worshipped in the Temple night and day, with fastings and prayers. Enlightened from on high, she also echoed

Simeon's canticle glorifying God, speaking of Jesus "to all who were awaiting the redemption of Jerusalem."

(Luke 2:38)

Patrick R. Moran: *Day by Day with the Saints* — Oct. 8

According to Scripture, Simeon lived in Jerusalem and was a just and devout man. Imbued with the Holy Spirit Simeon was told that he should not die until he had seen "the anointed of the Lord." According to custom, Mary and Joseph brought the Child Jesus into the Temple. Simeon took the Child into his arms, blessed Him and praised God.

He said, "Lord, now lettest thou thy servant depart in peace, according to thy word; for mine eyes have seen thy salvation, which thou hast prepared in the presence of all peoples, a light for revelation to the Gentiles, and for the glory of thy people Israel."   (Lk 2:29-32)

Joseph and Mary were pleased at what was said about the Child. Simeon blessed them and said to Mary, "Behold this child is set for the fall and the rising of many in Israel, and for a sign that is spoken against (and a sword will pierce through your own soul also), that thoughts out of many hearts may be revealed."   (Lk 2:34-35)

4. MEDITATION

It was probably a very ordinary day in the routine of the Temple when a poor family from the outskirts of Bethlehem arrived for the presentation and the purification ceremonies. Nothing special. No doubt hundreds of little families appeared that week, and some over-worked priest presided routinely over the rite.

But how easily people can misjudge. This was a very special family in which the child was the Son of God and the mother was pure above and beyond the prescriptions of the Law. Neither one needed the ceremonies to which they submitted. St. Luke is pointing out that the Holy Family was a good and God-fearing family, devoted to the fulfillment of the Law. Indeed, the Law was fulfilled in Christ, completed and finalized.

St. Paul points this out when he writes that the "plan he [God] was pleased to decree in Christ, to be carried out in the fullness of time" (Ephesians 1:10), was the fulfillment of all the promises made in the Old Testament. He adds, "But when the designated time had come, God sent forth his Son, born of a woman, born under the Law, to deliver from the Law those who were subjected to it, so that we might achieve our status as adopted sons." (Galatians 4:4-5)

At the Presentation Christ enters the Temple for the first time where He would later proclaim it "His Father's house," as we shall see in the next mystery of the Rosary. How often he would return to teach in this place! His presence gave it a dignity that made it greater than Solomon's Temple. (Malachi 3:1)

The Nunc Dimittis of Simeon is a canticle of praise to the God who has fulfilled all his promises to Israel. In fact, it is a prophetic re-weaving of three verses of promises from the prophet Isaiah. It also mentions, at the beginning of Christ's life, that His message is not only for the Chosen Race, but for all the Gentiles, the un-circumcised, the whole world.

The "sword of sorrow" that will pierce Mary's soul has been the object of the writings of many of the Fathers and Doctors of the Church, as well as many lesser-known authors. The "sign of con-tradiction" is undoubtedly the cross and the crucifixion, which has been a stumbling block to many. (1 Corinthians 1:23; Galatians 5:11; 1 Peter 2:8)

Among the many personal lessons we can draw from this mystery is loyalty to the law of God, especially as it presents itself in the duties of our own state in life. So many people still look for romantic or exotic or heroic ways to serve God, when the wonder and glory of it all starts with the simple and ordinary, everyday works of our lives.

The good and faithful servant who is faithful in little things, can hope for the help of God in being faithful in heroic things if they ever present themselves.

* * * * * * *   o   * * * * * * *   o   * * * * * * *

V.
Fifth Joyful Mystery
THE FINDING OF THE CHILD JESUS
IN THE TEMPLE

1. SCRIPTURE

His parents used to go every year to Jerusalem for the feast of the Passover, and when he was twelve they went up for the celebration as was their custom. As they were returning at the end of the feast, the child Jesus remained behind unknown to his parents. Thinking he was in the party, they continued their journey for a day, looking for him among their relatives and acquaintances.

Not finding him, they returned to Jerusalem in search of him. On the third day they came upon him in the temple, sitting in the midst of the teachers, listening to them and asking them questions. All who heard him were amazed at his intelligence and his answers.

When his parents saw him they were astonished, and his mother said to him: "Son, why have you done this to us? You see that your father and I have been searching for you in sorrow." He said to them: "Why did you search for me? Did you not know I had to be in my Father's house?" But they did not grasp what he said to them.

He went down with them then, and came to Nazareth, and was obedient to them. His mother meanwhile kept all these things in memory. Jesus, for his part, progressed steadily in wisdom and age and grace before God and man.   Luke 2:41-52   (NAB)

And he went down with them and came to Nazareth, and was subject to them; and his mother kept all these things carefully in her heart. And Jesus advanced in wisdom and age and grace before God and men.   Luke 2:51-52   (CCD)

He went down with them and came to Nazareth and lived under their authority. His mother stored up all these things in her heart. And Jesus increased in wisdom, in stature, and in favor with God and with people.
                                        Luke 2:51-52   (NJB)

Three times a year you shall celebrate a pilgrim feast to me. You shall keep the feast of the Unleavened Bread. As I have commanded you, you must eat unleavened bread for seven days at the prescribed time in the month of Abib, for it was then that you came out of Egypt. No one shall appear before me empty-handed.   Exodus 23:14-15   (NAB)

He told those who were selling doves: "Get them out of here! Stop turning my Father's house into a marketplace!" His disciples recalled the words of Scripture: "Zeal for your house consumes me" [Psalm 69:10]. John 2:16-17   (NAB)

The Jews were filled with amazement and said, "How did this man get his education when he had no teacher?"   John 7:15   (NAB)

"In my Father's house there are many dwelling places; otherwise, how could I have told you that I was going to prepare a place for you?"   John 14:2   (NAB)

2. ANCIENT AUTHORS

St. Bernard: *First Homily — Missus Est*

Mary calls Him "Son," who is the God and Lord of the Angels, saying "Son, why have You done this to us?" What Angel would dare say this! They consider it a rare privilege, being spirits, simply to be His messengers and do His bidding, as David affirms. "He has created spiritual beings to be His messengers."

Mary, recognizing her position as his Mother, did not hesitate to call Him "Son" whom the Angels serve in reverence. Nor did God hesitate to respond to the name and to revere the maternal majesty He had bestowed on her.

A little further on the evangelist says, "And He was subject to them." Who was subject to whom? God was subject to man! The God who commands all the orders of Angels was subject to Mary.

Which shall we admire first? The tremendous submission of the Son of God, or the tremendous God-given dignity of the Mother of God? Both are marvels; both amazing.

When God obeys a woman, it is humility without precedent. When a woman commands her God, it is sublime beyond measure. In praising virgins we read that they follow the Lamb wherever He goes. How can we possibly praise sufficiently the Virgin who leads Him?

Learn, O man, to obey; learn, O earth, to be subject; learn, O dust, to bow down. In speaking of your Creator, the evangelist says, "He was subject to them." Blush, proud ashes, for God humiliates Himself and you exalt yourself. God submits to men, but you, ignoring His example, seek to dominate your fellow men.

O Blessed Mary! You lack neither humility nor virginity. And it is a truly remarkable virginity which did not fear, but rather honored, fruitfulness. No less singular is the humility which did not suffer, indeed was exalted by the fruitful virginity.

Which of these is not marvelous or incomparable? Which one is not singular? The wonder is that we do not stop to contemplate! What is more worthy of admiration, the fruitfulness of the virgin or the integrity of the Mother; the divine dignity of the Child or the humility of the Sublime Infant?

Perhaps it is preferable, since each party is so incomparably excellent, each part more inspiring than the last, that the mystery be contemplated as a whole.

We certainly should not be surprised that God, Who is blessed and wonderful in His saints, should be yet more marvelous in His Mother. Virgins may praise the motherhood of this Virgin; the married may honor the virginity of this Mother. All men can imitate the humility of the Mother of God.

3. Recent Authors

Abbot Columba Marmion: *Christ in His Mysteries*

The Gospel has preserved for us only one episode of this period of Christ's life: the Child lost in the Temple.

You know the circumstances that had taken the Holy Family to Jerusalem. The Child Jesus was twelve years old. It was the age when young Israelites began to be subject to the precepts of the Mosaic Law, notably that of going to the Temple three times a year, at the feasts of the Passover, of Pentecost and of Tabernacles.

Our divine Savior who had willed, by His Circumcision, to bear the yoke of the Law, went then with Mary and His foster-father to the Holy City. It was doubtless the first time He had made the pilgrimage.

When this Boy entered into the Temple, none suspected that He was the God who was there adored. Jesus was there mingling with the crowd of Israelites, taking part in the ceremonies of the worship and in the chanting of the psalms. He understood, as none other ever will, the significance of the sacred rites and the symbolism of this liturgy which God Himself had laid down in detail.

At the time of the Passover, the throng of Jews was very considerable, and in returning, the caravans cannot have been easy to form, so it was not until late in the day that their composition could be recognized. Mary believed that Jesus was with Joseph, but what was her sorrowful surprise when, upon rejoining the group where Joseph was, she did not find the Child.

When she lost Jesus, Mary knew the sharp sufferings which were to increase her capacity of love and the extent of her merits. We can hardly measure the greatness of this affliction. But Mary knew Jesus too well to think that He had left them without some purpose.

The Child must now be sought. What days those were! God permitted that our Lady should be in darkness during those anxious hours. Mary and Joseph returned to Jerusalem with troubled hearts. The Gospel tells us that they looked for Jesus everywhere among their kinsfolk and acquaintances. Finally they found Him in the Temple, sitting in the midst of the doctors of the Law.

The doctors of Israel assembled in one of the halls of the Temple to explain the Holy Scriptures. Anyone might

come to join and listen, as Jesus did. He came into the midst
of them, not to teach — His hours for that would come —
but as one who was "hearing them and asking them questions." And the doctors of Israel, "were astonished at His
wisdom and His answers."

Mary and Joseph, overjoyed at finding Jesus, drew near
to Him and His Mother said, "Son, why have You done this
to us?" It is not a reproach, but it is the heart betraying its
maternal feelings. "Your father and I have sought You,
sorrowing."

And what is Christ's answer? "Why did you seek me?
Did you not know that I must be about my Father's
business?"

These are the first words to come from the lips of the
Incarnate Word as gathered up by the Gospel. They
epitomize the whole Person and the work of Jesus; they tell
of His divine Sonship and indicate His supernatural mission. All Christ's existence will be but a striking and magnificent commentary on these words.

Pope Paul VI: *Sermon at Nazareth* (1964)

Nazareth is a kind of school where we may discover
what Christ's life was really like, and even to understand His
gospel. Here we can observe and ponder the simple appeal
of the way God's Son came to be known, profound yet full of
hidden meaning.

Here we can sense and take account of the conditions
and circumstances that surrounded and affected His life on
earth — the places, the tenor of the times, the culture, the
language, religious customs and, in brief, everything which
Jesus used to make himself known to the world.

Father Leopold Sabourin, S.J.: *Christology: Basic Texts in Focus*

The first words of Jesus recorded in the Gospel are found in answer to Mary's question in the temple: "He said to them, 'How is it that you sought me? Did you not know that I must be in my Father's house?' " Taken literally, the Greek "in the (things) of my Father," seems at first sight better rendered in the Jerusalem Bible, "Did you not know that I must be busy with my Father's affairs?" And the Vulgate supports "in the things which are my Father's."

Luke 2:49 is the only text where Jesus refers to God as His Father in the presence of Joseph himself, but of course, he does make the claim elsewhere. In Luke 2:49-50, the misunderstanding of Mary and Joseph does not concern his divine Sonship, in some way already revealed to them, but the manner in which that Sonship finds expression.

In these verses, for the first time, we see Jesus use the word "must." He must be about His Father's work, a "necessity" which Luke particularly emphasizes. Jesus in Luke sees His whole life, activity, and particularly His passion as unfolding in the light of God's will, comprehended as a "must."

Father Michael O'Carroll: *Theotokos*

The passage which ends Luke's infancy narrative gives us our only direct information on the life of Jesus between his infancy and his entry into public life. It records his first spoken words, and the first of the two sentences spoken to him by Mary in the New Testament — the second being, "They have no wine" (Jn 2:3).

Mary is given prominence by the evangelist. Though Joseph is present, she it is who questions him on the motive of his stay in the Temple. She it is who keeps these things "in her heart." This concluding reflection, taken with Luke's declared intention of setting down what had been delivered by "those who from the beginning were eyewitnesses and ministers of the word" (Lk 1:2), lends probability to the opinion that in some way the story came from Mary.

4. MEDITATION

Once again the Holy Family is just an inconspicuous part of a devout Jewish throng who appear before the Lord on a Passover feast. They are fulfilling the law of the Lord with commendable piety.

This was probably Our Lord's first return to the Temple since the Presentation, and, as might be expected of a young Jew, he was impressed, even overwhelmed by the glories of the Temple and all that it signified. That he would be tempted to stay and give his whole life to God could be expected.

But of course, He was more than just an impressionable young fellow and Joseph and Mary knew that. When He was missing from the returning caravan, they probably had very divided hearts as they rushed back to Jerusalem. The first and natural thought would be, "What could have happened to Him?" All parental hearts fear the worst in an emergency.

But since they knew His origin, did they perhaps think that He was about to go public, begin His work, overcome with a sort of Divine impatience? Their common sense would have told them it was premature. Even when He finally began, He was only about thirty, and considered almost too young to be a Teacher in Israel.

They must have suspected that it was in some way connected with the reason for his birth, but the suspense must have been awful. Indeed, it was the occasion to drive home to Mary and Joseph, and through them to us, that He was always conscious of the purpose of His Incarnation — to do the work of His Father, God.

And after the lesson was taught, He went back to Nazareth and was subject to them. I think St. Bernard's meditation on that phrase,

"*He was subject to them,*" sums up completely all the patristic comment on this passage. On the devotional level, could we ask for a more dramatic lesson on humility and obedience?

The saints also love that small phrase, that Mary kept all these things in her heart, pondering over them, meditating about them. Any mother can tell you in detail, example after example, of the things her children did and said as they were growing up. She can go on for hours, with very little prompting.

Mary knew a bigger and greater secret about her Son. How she must have pondered all of His words and deeds, seeing in them the fulfillment of prophecy and the harbinger of things to come. It seems compelling to me, that Mary was the source of St. Luke's infancy narrative, even though modern critics like to discount that. I think the details are too clear and too genuine to have come to him second or third hand. Mary treasured these things in her heart!

That thought gives us new perspective on devotion to the Immaculate Heart of Mary. What treasures were stored there!

PART TWO

THE
SORROWFUL MYSTERIES

* * * * * *   ○   * * * * * * *   ○   * * * * *

* * * * * * * ○ * * * * * * ○ * * * * * *

VI.

First Sorrowful Mystery:
THE AGONY IN THE GARDEN

1. SCRIPTURE

Then Jesus went with them to a place called Gethsemane. He said to his disciples, "Stay here while I go over there and pray." He took along Peter and Zebedee's two sons, and began to experience sorrow and distress. Then he said to them, "My heart is nearly broken with sorrow. Remain here and stay awake with me."

He advanced a little and fell prostrate in prayer. "My Father, if it is possible, let this cup pass me by. Still let it be as you would have it, not as I." When he returned to his disciples he found them asleep. He said to Peter, "So you could not stay awake with me for even an hour? Be on guard and pray that you may not undergo the test. The spirit is willing but nature is weak."

Withdrawing a second time, he began to pray: "My Father, if this cannot pass me by without my drinking it, your will be done!" Once more on his return, he found them asleep; they could not keep their eyes open.

He left them again, withdrew somewhat, and began to pray a third time, saying the same words as before. Finally he returned to his disciples and said to them: "Sleep on now. Enjoy your rest! The hour is on us when the Son of Man is to be handed over to the power of evil men. Get up! Let us be on our way! See, my betrayer is here."

Matthew 26:36-46   (NAB)

And they went to a place which was called Gethsemane and he said to his disciples, "Sit here while I pray." And he took with him Peter and James and John, and began to be greatly distressed and troubled. And he said to them, "My soul is very sorrowful, even to death, remain here and watch." And going a little farther, he fell on the ground and prayed that, if it were possible, the hour might pass from him.

And he said, "Abba, Father, all things are possible to thee; remove this cup from me; yet not what I will, but what thou wilt." And he came and found them sleeping and he said to Peter, "Simon, are you asleep? Could you not watch one hour? Watch and pray that you may not enter into temptation; the spirit indeed is willing, but the flesh is weak."

And again he went and prayed, saying the same words. And again he came and found them sleeping, for their eyes were very heavy; and they did not know what to answer him.

And he came the third time and said to them, "Are you still sleeping and taking your rest? It is enough; the hour has come; the Son of man is betrayed into the hands of sinners. Rise, let us be going now, my betrayer is at hand."

Mark 14:32-42   (RSV)

And now he went out, as his custom was, to mount Olivet, his disciples following him. When he reached the place, he said to them, "Pray that you may not enter into temptation." Then he parted from them, going a stone's throw off, and knelt down to pray.

"Father," he said, "if it please thee, take away this chalice from before me; only as thy will is, not as mine is." And he had sight of an angel from heaven, encouraging him. And now he was in an agony, and prayed still more earnestly; his sweat fell to the ground like thick drops of blood.

When he rose from prayer, he went back to his disciples and found that they were sleeping, overwrought with sorrow. "How can you sleep?" he asked. "Rise up and pray, so that you may not enter into temptation."

Luke 22:39-46   (Knox)

Jesus explained to them: "Doing the will of him who sent me and bringing his work to completion is my food."

John 4:34   (NAB)

"But the world must know that I love the Father and do as the Father has commanded me."   John 14:31   (NAB)

After this discourse, Jesus went out with his disciples accross the Kidron Valley. There was a garden there, and he and his disciples entered it. The place was familiar to Judas as well (the one who was to hand him over) because Jesus had often met there with his disciples. John 18:1-2   (NAB)

> Though he was in the form of God,
> he did not deem equality with God
> something to be grasped at.
>
> Rather, he emptied himself
> and took the form of a slave,
> being born in the likeness of men.

He was known to be of human estate,
and it was thus that he humbled himself,
obediently accepting even death,
death on a cross!   Philippians 2:6-9   (NAB)

In the days when he was in the flesh, he offered prayers and supplications with loud cries and tears to God, who was able to save him from death, and he was heard because of his reverence. Son though he was, he learned obedience from what he suffered; and when perfected, he became the source of eternal salvation for all who obey him, designated by God as high priest according to the order of Melchizedek.

Hebrews 5:7-10   (NAB)

Then he says,
"I have come to do your will."

Hebrews 10:9   (NAB)

2. Ancient Authors

St. Cyprian: *The Good of Patience*

Jesus Christ, our Lord and our God, did not teach by words only, but He also fulfilled the teaching by His deeds. And He who said that He came down for this purpose, namely to do the will of His Father, among the other miracles of power by which He gave proof of His divine majesty, also preserved and exemplified His Father's patience by His habitual forbearance.

Accordingly, His every act right from the very outset of His coming is marked by an accompanying patience. From the first moment of His descent from the sublimity of heavenly to earthly things, He did not disdain, though the Son of God, to put on man's flesh, and although He Himself was not a sinner, to bear the sins of others. Having put aside His immortality for a time, He suffered Himself to become mortal, in order that, though innocent, He might be slain for the salvation of the guilty.

The Lord was baptized by His servant, and He, although destined to grant the remission of sins, did not disdain to have His body cleansed with the water of the Jordan. He, through whom others are fed, fasted for forty days. He felt hunger and starvation so that those who were famished for the word of God and grace might be filled with the Bread of Heaven.

He did not rule His disciples as a master rules his slaves, but being both kind and gentle, He loved them as a brother, even deigning to wash the feet of His apostles, that He might teach by His example. We should not wonder, then, that He was such a one who was able to tolerate Judas even to the end, with enduring patience.

In the very hour of His passion and death, before they had come to the cruel act of His slaughter and the shedding of blood, what violent abuses He listened to with patience and what shameful insults He endured! He was even covered with the spittle of His revilers when, but a short time before, with His own spittle, He had cured the eyes of the man born blind.

He who now crowns martyrs with eternal garlands was himself crowned with thorns. He who clothes all others with the garment of immortality was stripped of His earthly garment. He who has offered us the cup of salvation was given vinegar to drink. He the innocent, He the just, He who is innocence itself and justice itself, is counted among the criminals.

The Word of God, silent, is led to the cross. And although the stars are confounded at the crucifixion of the Lord, the elements are disturbed, the earth trembles, night

blots out the day, the sun withdraws its rays and its eyes lest it
be forced to gaze upon this crime, yet He does not speak,
nor is He moved, nor does He proclaim His majesty, even
during the suffering itself. He endures all things, even to the
end, with a constant perseverance so that in Christ, a full and
perfect patience may find its realization.

St. John Chrysostom: *Homily #47 on John*

Why, then, did He say: "Have I not chosen you, the
Twelve? Yet one of you is a devil"? To show that His teaching was not in any way colored by flattery. Since they alone
remained after all had left Him, and they were acknowledg-
ing through Peter that He was the Christ, in order that they
might not think that on this account He was going to cater to
them, He did away with the possibility of their entertaining
this notion.

What He meant is something like this: "Nothing keeps
me from reproving the wicked; do not think that because
you have remained with Me I shall not find fault with you if
you have done wrong." God is not wont to make people
good by compulsion and force, and His election and choice
are not coercive of those called, but rather, persuasive. And
that you may learn that the vocation does not coerce, consider how many of those called have been lost. It is plain
from this that salvation and damnation lie in the cooperation of our wills.

Therefore, when we hear these things, let us learn
always to be careful and vigilant. If Judas who was classed
among that saintly company, who had enjoyed so great a
gift, who had worked miracles, when he had become infected with the dread evil of greed, even betrayed his own
Master, and neither his good works nor his gifts helped him
— let us fear that we may imitate Judas by avarice.

You do not betray Christ? When you neglect a poor man wasted with hunger, or perishing with cold, you are liable to the same punishment as Judas. And when we partake of the Mysteries unworthily, we are lost in the same way as those who kill Christ. When we rob, when we despoil those weaker than we, we shall draw upon ourselves the greatest punishment.

3. RECENT AUTHORS

Father Peter J. Riga: *The Redeeming Christ*

The disciples could not understand the meaning of a suffering Messiah. Thus we can appreciate the great confusion and consternation of the disciples throughout the narration of the passion, for this was a crisis of their faith. They honestly believed that Jesus was the Messiah, but they could not reconcile this belief with the suffering and death, nor did the passion of Jesus fit their concept of the Messiah.

Jesus claimed to be from God; yet he suffered and died, and God did not come to his aid and save him. What the disciples expected and what they witnessed were diametrically opposed. The women were not so shaken in their faith because they adhered to him not by theory but by love. For this reason they did not abandon him when they did not understand what was happening.

There can be no understanding of the passion of Jesus without the resurrection of Jesus.

Mark stresses that the sorrow of Jesus in the garden was deep and abiding. "And he began to be greatly troubled and distressed." The word "troubled" means to be profoundly agitated, a ripping and tearing state of anguish. The word "distressed" indicates a strong state of upheaval and trouble.

This state overcomes Jesus to the point of having "his soul troubled even unto death." Jesus frequently speaks of his soul, and this expression can be found in the Old Testament as well. It means one's whole being and not the Greek idea of spiritual principle of man.

John Banister Tabb: *Recognition*

> When Christ went up to Calvary,
> His crown upon His head,
> Each tree unto its fellow tree
> In awful silence said:
> "Behold the gardener is He
> Of Eden and Gethsemane."

Joseph Mary Plunkett: *I See His Blood Upon The Rose*

> I see His Blood upon the rose,
> And in the stars the glory of His eyes.
> His body gleams amid the eternal skies.
>
> I see His face in every flower;
> The thunder, and the singing of the birds
> Are but His voice — and carven by His power,
> Rocks are His written words.
>
> All pathways by His feet are worn,
> His strong Heart stirs the ever-beating sea,
> His Crown of Thorns is twined with every thorn,
> His Cross is every tree.

U.S. Bishops' Pastoral Letter (1919)

The lot of the Negro and the Indian, though latterly much improved, is far from being what the Church would desire. Both have been hampered by adverse conditions. . . .

In the eyes of the Church there is no distinction of race or nation; these are human souls and these have all alike been purchased at the same great price, the Blood of Jesus Christ.

4. MEDITATION

The early Fathers and Doctors of the Church treated the great theological themes in the Passion and Death of Christ. The Paschal Mystery was at the heart of our economy of salvation and they considered the great themes of redemption, justification, salvation and atonement.

This was all a vital part of incarnational theology and the Christological crises that swept the Church after the centuries of proscription. Analysis of the various steps in the Paschal journey waited until later centuries when, the doctrinal battles settled, the devotional practices could grow on solid foundations.

In the agony of Christ in the Garden of Gethsemane (the olive press), later writers would see tremendous significance in the prayer of Christ, His perfect abandonment to the Will of His Father, and the sweating of Blood, the first that we know He shed since the Circumcision.

Books, articles, essays, poems and hymns have been written about each of these events, small against the great canvas of the Passion, Crucifixion and Resurrection, but large in the devotional life of the devout Christian.

In the language of love, in the movement of the heart, each step on the way to Calvary is precious. It is that saving and loving journey which is described in the Imitation of Christ *as "the royal road of the Cross." Christ has many who will share His joys and triumphs. Dedicated, indeed, are those who hasten to accompany Him along that road.*

O. Scarpelli

* * * * * * *   o   * * * * * * *   o   * * * * * * *

VII.

Second Sorrowful Mystery:
THE SCOURGING AT THE PILLAR

1. SCRIPTURE

As soon as it was daybreak the chief priests, with the elders and scribes (that is, the whole Sanhedrin), reached a decision. They bound Jesus, led him away, and handed him over to Pilate. Pilate interrogated him: "Are you the king of the Jews?" "You are the one who is saying it," Jesus replied. The chief priests, meanwhile, brought many accusations against him. Pilate interrogated him again: "Surely you have some answer? See how many accusations they are leveling against you." But greatly to Pilate's surprise, Jesus made no further response.

Now on the occasion of a festival he would release for them one prisoner — any man they asked for. There was a prisoner named Barabbas jailed along with the rebels who had committed murder in the uprising. When the crowd came up to press their demand that he honor the custom, Pilate rejoined, "Do you want me to release the king of the Jews for you?" He was aware, of course, that it was out of jealousy that the chief priests had handed him over.

Meanwhile, the chief priests incited the crowd to have him release Barabbas instead. Pilate again asked them, "What am I to do with the man you call the king of the Jews?" They shouted back, "Crucify him!" Pilate protested, "Why? What crime has he committed?" They only shouted the louder, "Crucify him!"

So Pilate, who wished to satisfy the crowd, released Barabbas to them; and after he had had Jesus scourged, he handed him over to be crucified.   Mark 15:1-15   (NAB).

Pilate finally realized that he was making no impression and that a riot was breaking out instead. He called for water and washed his hands in front of the crowd, declaring as he did so, "I am innocent of the blood of this just man. The responsibility is yours." The whole people said in reply, "Let his blood be on us and on our children."

At that, he released Barabbas to them. Jesus, however, he first had scourged; then he handed him over to be crucified.   Matthew 27:24-26   (NAB)

Pilate's next move was to take Jesus and have him scourged.   John 19:1   (NAB)

Who would believe what we have heard?
    To whom has the arm of the Lord been
        revealed?
He grew up like a sapling before him,
    like a shoot from the parched earth;
There was in him no stately bearing to make us look
        at him,
    nor appearance that would attract us to him.
He was spurned and avoided by men,
    a man of suffering, accustomed to infirmity.
One of those from whom men hide their faces,
    spurned, and we held him in no esteem.

Yet it was our infirmities that he bore,
  our suffering that he endured.
While we thought of him as stricken,
  as one smitten by God and afflicted.
But he was pierced for our offenses,
  crushed for our sins;
Upon him was the chastisement that makes us
        whole,
  by his stripes we were healed.
We had all gone astray like sheep,
  each following his own way;
But the Lord laid upon him
  the guilt of us all.
Though he was harshly treated, he submitted
  and opened not his mouth;
Like a lamb led to the slaughter
  or a sheep before the shearers,
  he was silent and opened not his mouth.

                              Isaiah 53:1-7   (NAB)

2. ANCIENT AUTHORS

St. Basil: *Homily on Psalm 44*

"You are ripe in beauty, above the sons of men."

                                       Psalm 44:3

Now David calls the Lord ripe in beauty above the sons of men when he fixes his gaze on His divinity. He does not celebrate the beauty of the flesh. "And we have seen Him, and He had no sightliness, nor beauty, but His appearance was without honor and lacking above the sons of men." It is evident then, that the prophet, looking upon His brilliance and being filled with the splendor there, his soul smitten

..rth this beauty, was moved to a divine love of the spiritual beauty, and when this appeared to the human soul all things beside that seemed shameful and abominable.

Therefore, even St. Paul, when he saw His ripe beauty, "counted all things as dung that he might gain Christ." Those outside the word of truth, despising the simplicity of expression in the Scriptures, call the preaching of the Gospel folly; but we who glory in the cross of Christ know that the grace poured out by God in the teachings concerning Christ is rich.

The saying of Paul to the Philippians is also much like this: "He humbled Himself, becoming obedient to death, even on a cross. Therefore God has exalted Him." It is clear that these words are spoken concerning the Savior as a man.

St. Clement of Rome: *Letter to the Corinthians*

For Christ belongs to the humble-minded, not to those who exalt themselves above His flock. The scepter of the majesty of God, the Lord Jesus Christ, came not in pomp or arrogance, though He was mighty; but He was humble-minded as the Holy Spirit spoke concerning Him.

For He says, "Lord, who has believed our report, and to whom is the arm of the Lord revealed? We announced in His presence — He is as a child, as a sprout in thirsty ground. There is no beauty in Him, nor comeliness, and we have seen Him and He has neither form nor beauty."

You see, beloved, what is the example given to us. For if the Lord was thus humble-minded, what shall we do who through Him have come under the sway of His grace?

In charity, then, the Lord received us; out of the charity which He has for us, Jesus Christ our Lord gave His blood for us by the will of God, and His flesh for our flesh, and His life for our lives.

St. Athanasius: *On the Incarnation*

If anyone wants to know why He suffered death on the cross and not in some other way, we answer this: in no other way was it expedient for us; indeed, the Lord offered for our sake the one death that was supremely good. He had come to bear the curse that lay on us; and how could He become a curse otherwise than by accepting the accursed death? And that death is the cross, for it is written "Cursed is every one that hangs on a tree."

Again, the death of the Lord is the ransom of all, and by it "the middle wall of partition" is broken down and the call of the Gentiles comes about. How could He have called us if He had not been crucified, for it is only in the cross that a man dies with arms outstretched? Here, again, we see the fitness of the death and of those outstretched arms; it was that He might draw his ancient people with the one and the Gentiles with the other and join both together in Himself.

Jacopone da Todi: *Stabat Mater*, v.4

> Bruised, derided, cursed, defiled,
> She beheld her tender child
> All with bloody scourges rent;
> For the sins of His own nation,
> Saw Him hang in desolation,
> Till His Spirit forth He sent.

MODERN AUTHORS

Archbishop Alban Goodier, S.J.: *The Passion and Death of Our Lord Jesus Christ*

Jesus, the way, the truth and the life, who had done all things well, whom no man could convict of any sin, of whom

His enemies had said that for his good works they accused
him not, was delivered over to the servants of the law. There
was now nothing left to be done but for the preliminaries of
the execution to begin.

First He must be scourged because such was the ordinary treatment of one condemned to death. But in the
scourging, Jesus, the Son of David was not to enjoy the
benefit of the Jewish Law. According to that Law, even in
the worst cases, scourging was confined to "forty stripes, less
one" (Deut 25:2-3).

The Roman Law had no such limits; moreover, the
prisoner was not a Roman citizen, a title which alone would
have saved Him from such degradation. He was only a Jew,
only a Galilean, only one of those hill-country people who
were forever giving trouble. He was one of those on whom
these Roman soldiers could vent their cruelty and contempt
to their heart's content.

The evangelists, one and all, pass the scene over, either
because there had been no witness to give them the details,
or, more probably, because the scene was too terrible, too
horrible, too painful to be described. But Jesus Himself had
not passed it over. Again and again in His prophecies of the
Passion He had come back to it, as if from the beginning it
had been something from which His human nature had
shrunk (Mt 22:18-19; Mk 10:33-34; Lk 18:32-33).

At the command of both Jews and Romans, Jesus
Christ was stripped of His clothing; He was tied to a whip-
ping post; He was beaten till His whole Body became one
gaping wound, till it fell exhausted to the ground, till
brutalized men, brought up to cruelty, revelling in it as
sport, boasting of it as if it were a mark of bravery, restricted
to no limit, were satisfied.

Jesus Christ, the Son of God, was left in their hands that
they might vent their brutality upon Him unrestrained.

Frank J. Sheed: *What Difference Does Jesus Make?*

The Evangelists do not luxuriate in horrors. We know, for example, what a Roman scourging was: merely reading the details can turn the stomach. But we do not read them in the Gospels.

We are simply told that Pilate had Him scourged, and then presented the scourged man to the crowd as a reason against bothering to go on with the crucifixion. His "Ecce Homo" could only have meant, "Look at him now." Jesus must have been blood-bathed, but none of them mentions blood till he is dead.

They do not utter their own feelings, as he does not utter his. He complained of nothing, he blamed no one, judged no one, was wholly judged.

Everyone must read the four accounts for himself. I can only record my own impression — that he allowed none of the tortures he suffered as Victim to disturb his central concentration on what he was doing as Priest for the redemption of the whole human race.

Father Walter Farrell, O.P.: *Companion to the Summa*

What Christ suffered was every *kind* of suffering. His passion was the work of Jews and Gentiles, of men and women, of princes and their officials, of priests and people, of friends and enemies. What can a man suffer? Well, he can be deserted by friends. He can be stripped of his reputation, robbed of respect and honor. He can lose his possessions, even his very clothes. His soul can be weighed down by the weariness of distaste, by fear, by sorrow. His body can be beaten and wounded. It was in this sense of a man utterly stripped that Christ hung naked on the cross.

He suffered every manner of suffering and His sufferings were greater in intensity than any other the world has ever seen. It is quite possible that some other man was scourged longer, was crowned with thorns sharper, or carried a heavier cross. The question here is not of this or that suffering, but of all these sufferings taken together in a subject Who was the Son of God.

Christ insisted that every one of His faculties operate to its fullest for the redemption of man. All this suffering was in the most complete sense *voluntary*. He took upon Himself the amount and degree of suffering proportionate to the fruit that suffering was expected to bear — nothing less than the redemption of all men from all sin.

4. MEDITATION

The Gospels are so matter-of-fact about the scourging at the pillar that a casual reading might let us pass it by. In view of the death by crucifixion, it seems only a matter of a prelude, one that deserves a passing glance and that's all.

But the fact that our Lord always referred to the two together gives it a deeper significance. Many a slave died under the lash of the Roman executioners long before they set out for their crucifixion. One can only shudder to think of the kind of man who became a deliberate torturer. The brutality of action and the cast of mind that supported it are monstrous, to say the least.

Yet Christ underwent this cruelty as part of His total act of love. He not only loved so much that He willingly put His life on the line in place of ours, but He allowed the death to be as cruel as possible. No one can ever doubt the totality of His act of love.

In human love songs we sing of climbing the highest mountains and swimming the deepest oceans to prove our love, because we know talk is cheap. It is easy to say "I love you"; it's another thing to prove that love.

The power of these sorrowful mysteries of the Rosary is that they make us ponder, in detail, how infinitely perfect was Christ's love for us. We come to the inescapable conclusion that this Divine Love has been poured out for us and in us. We also have to face the fact of both the reality of sin and its enormity.

* * * * * * * o * * * * * * o * * * * * *

VIII.
Third Sorrowful Mystery:
THE CROWNING WITH THORNS

1. SCRIPTURE

The procurator's soldiers took Jesus inside the praetorium and collected the whole cohort around him. they stripped off his clothes and wrapped him in a scarlet military cloak. Weaving a crown out of thorns they fixed it on his head, and stuck a reed in his right hand. Then they began to mock him by dropping to their knees before him, saying, "All hail, king of the Jews!" They also spat at him. Afterward they took hold of the reed and kept striking him on the head. Finally, when they had finished making a fool of him, they stripped him of the cloak, dressed him in his own clothes, and led him off to crucifixion.

Matthew 27:27-31   (NAB)

The soldiers now led Jesus away into the hall known as the praetorium; at the same time they assembled the whole cohort. They dressed him in royal purple, then wove a crown of thorns and put it on him, and began to salute him, "All hail King of the Jews!" Continually striking Jesus on the

head with a reed and spitting at him, they genuflected
before him and pretended to pay him homage. When they
had finished mocking him, they stripped him of the purple,
dressed him in his own clothes, and led him out to crucify
him.   Mark 15:16-20   (NAB)

Pilate's next move was to take Jesus and have him
scourged. The soldiers then wove a crown of thorns and
fixed it on his head, throwing around his shoulders a cloak
of royal purple. Repeatedly they came up to him and said,
"All hail, king of the Jews!" slapping his face as they did so.

Pilate went out a second time and said to the crowd:
"Observe what I do. I am going to bring him out to you to
make you realize that I find no case against him." When
Jesus came out wearing the crown of thorns and the purple
cloak, Pilate said to them, "Look at the man!" As soon as the
chief priests and the temple guards saw him they shouted,
"Crucify him! Crucify him!"   John 19:1-6   (NAB)

And I have not rebelled,
    have not turned back.
I gave my back to those who beat me,
    my cheeks to those who plucked my beard;
My face I did not shield
    from buffets and spitting.
                                    Isaiah 50:5-6   (NAB)

If he gives his life as an offering for sin,
    he shall see his descendants in a long life,
        and the will of the Lord shall be accomplished
            through him.
Because of his affliction
    he shall see the light in fullness of days;

Through his suffering, my servant shall justify
  many,
  and their guilt he shall bear.
Therefore I will give him his portion among the
  great,
  and he shall divide the spoils with the mighty,
Because he surrendered himself to death
  and was counted among the wicked;
And he shall take away the sins of many,
  and win pardon for their offenses.

Isaiah 53:10-12 (NAB)

2. ANCIENT AUTHORS

St. Bonaventure: *The Breviloquium*

Now concerning the nature of Christ's suffering, this must be said. Christ suffered a passion most comprehensive, most bitter, and most shameful, a passion deadly, yet life-giving. Even though he could not suffer in His divine nature, He suffered in His human nature a passion most comprehensive, for not only every part of His body was affected, but every power of soul as well.

He suffered a passion most bitter, for besides enduring the anguish of His wounds, He endured the added anguish of grieving for our sins. He suffered a passion most shameful, alike because crucifixion was a punishment set aside for the worst criminals, and because He was placed in the company of evildoers, that is robbers: He was counted among the wicked.

He also suffered a passion that was deadly, for it separated body and soul, although both remained united with the Godhead. Wrong, indeed, is he who says that the Son of God ever relinquished the nature He had assumed.

As the Creator had created man in an orderly fashion, so must the Redeemer redeem him in an orderly fashion. He must restore him in such a way as to respect not only the freedom of the will, but also the honor of God and the harmonious functioning of the universe.

Christ, therefore, restored man through His all-efficacious example. An example is all-efficacious when it both invites to the summit of virtue and shows the way there. Now, nothing could show man the way of virtue more clearly than the example of a death endured for the sake of divine justice and obedience: a death, moreover, not of the ordinary sort, but agonizing in the extreme.

Nothing could move man to virtue more strongly than the merciful love with which the most high Son of God laid down His life for us who were not only undeserving, but actually full of guilt. This merciful love appears all the greater in that the sufferings He endured for us, indeed, willed to endure, were so cruel and so humiliating.

Then how could God who has not spared even His own Son but has delivered Him for us all . . . fail to grant us also all things with Him? We are invited, then, to love Him, and loving Him, to follow His example.

St. Gregory Nazianzen: *Fourth Theological Oration*

"He learnt obedience by the things which He suffered," and to His "strong crying and tears," and His "entreaties," and His "being heard," and His "reverence," all of which He wondrously wrought out, like a drama whose plot was devised on our behalf.

For in His character as the Word He was neither obedient nor disobedient. Such expressions belong to servants and inferiors, and the one applies to the better sort of them, while the other belongs to those who deserve punishment.

But in the character of the Form of a Servant, He condescends to His fellow-servants, nay, to His servants, and takes upon Him a strange form, bearing all me and mine in Himself, that in Himself He may exhaust the bad, as fire does wax or as the sun does the mists of earth; and that I may partake of His nature by His work.

Thus He honors obedience by His actions, and proves it experimentally by His Passion. For to possess the disposition is not enough, just as it would not be enough for us, unless we also proved it by our acts; action is the proof of disposition.

And, perhaps it would not be wrong to assume this also, that by the act of His love for us He gauges our obedience, and measures all by comparison with His own sufferings, so that He may know our conditions by His own, and how much is demanded of us, and how much we yield, taking into account, of course, our environment and our weakness also.

3. RECENT AUTHORS

H.W. Baker: *O Sacred Head*

O Sacred Head, surrounded
By crown of piercing thorn.
O bleeding Head, so wounded,
Reviled and put to scorn.
Our sins have marred the glory
Of your most holy Face,
Yet angel hosts adore You,
And tremble as they gaze.

The Lord of every nation
Was hung upon a tree;
His death was our salvation,
Our sins, His agony.
O Jesus, by Your Passion,
Your life in us increase;
Your death for us did fashion
Our pardon and our peace.

Archbishop Alban Goodier, S.J.: *The Passion and Death of Our Lord Jesus Christ*

The Roman soldiers stripped Jesus; this King must first be clothed in royal robes. They threw a scarlet cloak across His naked and scarred shoulders, some cast-off garment of an officer of the guard. They set Him against the wall, probably on a tub for a throne, Him of whom an angel had said, "The Lord shall give Him the throne of David His father and He shall reign in the house of Jacob forever" (Lk 1:32).

Yet so He was now enthroned and He must needs be crowned; with what should they crown Him. In a corner of the courtyard there was a heap of prickly bramble, put there to supply the fire. One of the soldiers had a happy idea.

He took his sword, cut away some of the twigs, beat them into a ball between his sword and his staff, for they were too thorny to be handled, and clamped them down upon the head of Jesus, hammering them till they fitted like a helmet.

Thus was Jesus crowned, seated on His throne of shame. The enthronement had suggested coronation; the crowning suggested a sceptre. There were rushes strewn about the floor, to serve as a carpet. Another soldier picked up one of these, and pushed it between the fettered hands, and behold, Jesus Christ, the King of the Jews, crowned in state in the very court of the Roman Pilate by Pilate's own bodyguard!

One idea followed another. The King had been crowned; He must now be duly honored by His courtiers and devoted subjects. They knew how this was done; often enough they had stood on guard when men had paid obeisance to monarchs, when local chiefs and petty kings had done homage to their overlord.

It was an easy thing for them to go through the mock ceremonial; what one did another imitated in solemn, derisive procession. "All hail! King of the Jews!" There was special bitterness in the choice of salutation they used. They showed contempt not only for Jesus but for all His race, as well.

As each soldier rose from his knee, he invented some new device, vying with those who had gone before him, by which he might pour ridicule and insult on the Man who sat, clothed in scarlet, crowned with thorns and with a sceptre in His hand, silent and unmoved against the wall of the court.

Despite all this, through the blood that blinded His eyes, He could look into the near future and know that the kingdom would be won.

Father Edward J. Mally, S.J.: *The Gospel According to Mark*

The soldiers referred to here are in the pay of the Romans and the incident took place inside the praetorium, the official designation of the place where the governor presided when he was in Jerusalem. It is commonly identified with the Fortress Antonia at the NW corner of the Temple precincts. A few think it was in Herod's palace, but the site is not crucial to the interpretation of this passage.

The whole cohort, depending on the translation of the Greek could be either 200 or 600 men. However, the "whole" cohort need not be taken strictly.

Matthew refers to a scarlet cloak but Mark mentions a purple military cloak, which is probably more exact. The purple is more symbolic of the royal dignity.

The crown of thorns could not have been woven in a wreath. The long thorns used for fires would have been stored in the courtyard, and they could easily be arranged in a radiate crown of the type worn by Hellenistic kings — familiar to us from its appearance on the Statue of Liberty.

"Hail! King of the Jews!" was a mockery that included a parody of imperial acclamations, "Ave, Caesar, victor, imperator!" It heightens the destiny of Jesus who draws from ordinary men only a lack of comprehension. To the soldiers he appears only as another prisoner and a means of idling away a weary hour: if you want to be a king, we'll make you one. It also brings out that it was as king of the Jews that Jesus suffered.

Joseph Benedict: *Rosary Mysteries*

While his enemies spent a busy night plotting his death, Christ was being tormented by the cruel Roman guards. He had said he was a king, so they made him a crown of thorns and pressed the terrible spikes into his head. Indeed, he took upon himself the price of our sins. "A man of sorrows . . . from whom men hide their faces. . . ." (Isaiah 53:3).

4. MEDITATION

The crowning with thorns seems to be just an act of added cruelty that tells us much of the temper of those times and the rigor of the Roman rule. It was so unnecessary, and so unnecessarily cruel.

But the symbolism cannot escape the Christian. Christ came in fulfillment of the prophecies to men like King David, that his rule would go on forever. Christ was of the royal race and lineage and He was to enter His triumph through the paschal mysteries.

The apostles and disciples wanted an earthly King-Messiah, but that was a pale image of the reality, of a divine King who could grant eternal life and liberty and happiness, not the temporary good times of a wise and strong earthly king. Such a crown was of no more use to Christ than the crown of thorns.

In this mystery we see that the contempt that Christ suffered came from both Jews and Gentiles. None of our ancestors are innocent, if we want to pursue that thought.

And if we want a modern application, we might examine ourselves for the prejudices we do have. In the contempt we show for others, we identify ourselves with those who mocked Christ. We can see Him in those who suffer from racism, sexism, opportunism, religious and economic intolerance, and oppression.

And the power of another mystery of the Rosary reaches out to us.

IX.

Fourth Sorrowful Mystery:
THE CARRYING OF THE CROSS

1. SCRIPTURE

On their way out they met a Cyrenian named Simon.
This man they pressed into service to carry the cross. Upon
arriving at a site called Golgotha (a name which means Skull
Place), they gave him a drink of wine flavored with gall,
which he tasted but refused to drink.

                                    Matthew 27:32-34   (NAB)

A man named Simon of Cyrene, the father of Alexander
and Rufus, was coming in from the fields, and they pressed
him into service to carry the cross. When they brought Jesus
to the site of Golgotha (which means "Skull Place"), they
tried to give him wine drugged with myrrh, but he would
not take it.   Mark 15:21-23   (NAB)

As they led him away, they laid hold of one Simon the
Cyrenian who was coming in from the fields. They put a
crossbeam on Simon's shoulder for him to carry along behind Jesus. A great crowd of people followed him, including
women who beat their breasts and lamented over him.

103

Jesus turned to them and said: "Daughters of Jerusalem, do not weep for me. Weep for yourselves and for your children. The days are coming when they will say, 'Happy are the sterile, the wombs that never bore and the breasts that never nursed.' Then they will begin saying to the mountains, 'Fall on us,' and to the hills, 'Cover us.' If they do these things in the green wood, what will happen in the dry?"   Luke 23:26-31   (NAB)

Jesus was led away, and carrying the cross by himself, went out to what is called the Place of the Skull (in Hebrew, *Golgotha*).   John 19:16-17   (NAB)

They cried out to the mountains and rocks, "Fall on us! Hide us from the face of the One who sits on the throne and from the wrath of the Lamb! The great day of vengeance has come. Who can withstand it?"

Revelation 6:16-17   (NAB)

The high places of Aven shall be destroyed, the sin of Israel; thorns and thistles shall overgrow their altars. Then shall they cry out to the mountains, "Cover us!" and to the hills, "Fall upon us!"   Hosea 10:8   (NAB)

2. ANCIENT AUTHORS

St. John Chrysostom: *Homilies on John*, #85

They placed the cross on Christ's shoulders as if on one accursed. Now this was also the case in type, for Isaac carried the wood for the sacrifice [cf. Genesis 22]. At that time, however, the sacrifice took place only insofar as being willed by the father (for it was merely a type), while now it was taking place in actuality, for it was the fulfillment of the type.

"And he came to the place called the Skull." Some say that there Adam had died and lay buried, and that Jesus set up His trophy over death in the place where death had begun its rule. For he went forth bearing His cross as a trophy in opposition to the tyranny of death, and, as is customary with conquerors, He also carried on His shoulders the symbol of His victory; no matter that the Jewish officials were here acting with an altogether different end in mind.

St. Cyril of Alexandria: *8th Sermon on the Passion*

How marvelous the power of the cross, how great beyond all telling the glory of the passion — here is the judgment seat of the Lord, the condemnation of the world, the supremacy of Christ crucified.

The different sacrifices of animals are no more. The one offering of Your Body and Blood is the fulfillment of all the different sacrificial offerings, for You are the true Lamb of God who takes away all the sins of the world. In You, Yourself, You bring to perfection all mysteries.

3. RECENT AUTHORS

St. Alphonsus Liguori: *The Glories of Mary*

While Mary was waiting at that place, she must have heard many things said about her beloved son by the members in the crowd who recognized her. Perhaps they even mocked her.

Alas, what a scene of sorrows then presented itself before her — the nails, the hammers, the cords, the fatal instruments of the death of her son, all of which were carried before him. And what a sword must the sound of that trumpet have been to her heart, the sound which proclaimed the sentence pronounced against her Jesus!

She raised her eyes and saw, O God! a young man covered with blood and wounds from head to foot, a wreath of thorns on his head, and two heavy beams on his shoulders. She looked at him and hardly recognized him, thinking, with Isaiah, "And we have seen him, and there was no comeliness in him" (Is 53:2).

Yes, for the wounds, the bruises, and the matted blood, gave him the appearance of a leper, so that he could no longer be known. "His look was, as it were, hidden and despised; whereupon we esteemed him not. We have thought of him as if he were a leper" (Is 53:3-4).

But at length love revealed him to her and as soon as she knew that it indeed was he, ah, what love and fear must have then filled her heart! On the one hand she wanted to see him, and on the other she dreaded so heartrending a sight. At length, they looked at each other.

The Son wiped the clotted blood from his eyes which had prevented him from seeing, and looked at his mother, and the Mother looked at her Son. Ah, looks of bitter grief, which, as so many arrows, pierced through and through those two beautiful and loving souls.

The Mother would have embraced him, but the guards thrust her aside with insults, and urged the suffering Lord forward. And Mary followed him. She followed him to Calvary where the sight of her dying Jesus was to cost her such bitter sorrow, but the loving Mary will not leave him.

And so the Son advanced, and the Mother followed, to be crucified with him. Let us pity her, but let us follow her by bearing with patience the crosses that Our Lord imposes on us. We have come to witness a new kind of martyrdom — a Mother condemned to see an innocent Son, and one whom she loves with the whole affection of her very being, cruelly tormented and put to death before her very eyes.

Archbishop Fulton J. Sheen: *Life of Christ*

The procession of the cross was usually preceded by a trumpeter to clear the road; then followed a herald announcing the name of the criminal who was being led to execution. Sometimes the name of the criminal and the reason for his condemnation was written on a board and hung about his neck.

Two witnesses of the council which sentenced the one condemned to death were also to accompany the procession. A centurion mounted on horseback, along with a considerable detachment of soldiers, formed part of the procession. There were also the two thieves who were to be crucified with Our Lord. He bore the full weight of the cross on His back and shoulders which were already raw from the scourging.

The Sunday previous He was hailed as "King"; that morning the people shouted: "No King but Caesar." The Jerusalem that saluted Him was now the Jerusalem that disowned Him.

Christ, the ultimate in sin offering (cf. Lev 16:27), is driven like the scapegoat outside the city. St. Paul suggests that from that moment the city forfeited its claim to greatness and was replaced by the heavenly Jerusalem (Heb 13:12-14).

Fearful that the long scourgings, the loss of blood, the crowning with thorns would bring His end before the crucifixion, His enemies compelled a stranger, Simon of Cyrene, to help Him carry His cross. Who was Simon? He could have been Jewish, judging by his name, or a Gentile; it may be that he was even a black African, judging by his native locality, and the fact that he was "forced" to help Our Lord carry the cross.

Father Josemaria Escriva: *The Way of the Cross*

Outside the city, to the north-west of Jerusalem, there is a little hill: Golgotha is its name in Aramaic; in Latin: the place of the skull or Calvary.

Offering no resistance, Jesus gives Himself up to the execution of the sentence. He is to be spared nothing, and upon His shoulders falls the weight of the ignominious cross. But through love, the cross is to become the throne from which he reigns.

The people of Jerusalem and those from abroad who have come for the Passover push their way through the city streets, to catch a passing glimpse of Jesus of Nazareth, the King of the Jews. There is a tumult of voices, and, now and then, short silences: perhaps when Jesus fixes His eyes on someone.

If anyone wishes to come after me, let him take up his cross daily and follow me (Matt. 16:24).

How lovingly Jesus embraces the wood which is to bring Him to death!

Is it not true that as soon as you cease to be afraid of the cross, of what people call the cross, when you set your will to accept the Will of God, then you find happiness, and all your worries, all your sufferings, physical or moral, pass away?

Truly, the cross of Jesus is gentle and lovable. There, sorrows cease to count; there is only the joy of knowing that we are co-redeemers with Him.

As if it were a festival, they have prepared an escort, a long procession. The judges want to savor their victory with a slow and pitiless torture.

Jesus is not to meet a quick death. . . . He is given time in which to prolong the identification of His pain and love with the most lovable Will of the Father. "I find My pleasure in doing Your Will, my God, and Your law dwells deep within My heart" (Ps. 39:9).

That voice you hear within you: "What a heavy yoke you have freely taken upon yourself!" is the voice of the devil; the heavy burden is our pride.

Ask Our Lord for humility, and you too will understand these words of Jesus, "For my yoke is sweet and my burden light" (Matt. 11:30) which I freely translate: My yoke is freedom, my yoke is love, my yoke is unity, my yoke is life, my yoke is fruitfulness.

B. Brown: *Way of the Cross* (edited)

One of the most familiar exercises of Christian piety, this is also known as the Stations of the Cross. It centers on 14 chosen representations of the sufferings of Christ on His way to Calvary. The devotion is practiced in imitation of the pilgrims who travel to the Holy Land to visit the places hallowed by Christ's sufferings.

As St. Jerome attests, pilgrimages to the Holy Land began in the earliest of Christian centuries. St. Brigid relates a vision in which she was told that the Blessed Mother visited these places after the Ascension.

When the Franciscans took custody of the shrines in the Holy Land in 1342, they took as part of their mission to promote devotions to these places and to the Passion of Christ. In the mid eighteenth century, St. Leonard of Port Maurice became the "Preacher of the Way of the Cross." With directions from Pope Clement XII in 1731, the fourteen stations as we commonly practice them became the norm. They combine scriptural incidents with local pious customs that were popular in the Middle Ages.

There is nothing to forbid popular devotion adding other stations or changing the number of them, or even the sequence, at least in private devotions.

In many places a fifteenth station has been added, the Resurrection.

4. MEDITATION

For those who perform the Way of the Cross regularly, or at least on the Fridays of Lent, this mystery is filled with imagery. From the moment Pilate hands Jesus over to the executioners we are accustomed to the high drama of the journey up to Calvary.

Jesus is made to carry the cross, and despite what some have written about Christ lovingly embracing the wood of the cross, that is hard to support from the scriptural evidence. He knew what the agony of that journey would be and how it would exhaust his human nature with its terrible pain. He seemed to have a special, human dread of the scourging at the pillar which preceded this awful passage.

It is a simple matter of deduction to meditate on the falls along the path, and to place them at three is a pious thought. Meeting His Mother, comforting in a prophetic way the weeping women, and the legend of Veronica add a special dimension to the human response to his suffering. That one of the weeping women would probably have offered a cloth or a towel seems logical and suitable, but whether it happened, certainly, and whether her name was Veronica cannot be sustained with any historical accuracy.

As a side thought, it is interesting to note that St. Charles Borromeo forbade the devotion to "St." Veronica in the Ambrosian rite in Milan.

The character and role of Simon the Cyrenian has always captivated the imagination of those who comment on the passage to Golgotha. The fact that his name is preserved and his sons' as well, suggests that, if he wasn't a follower of Christ before, he certainly became one later. There's a certain logic to that speculation that appeals to me. That he might have been a Black man is also an ancient speculation.

The stripping of Our Lord of His garments must have been particularly painful, since the bloody wounds must have adhered to the cloth. Whether Christ was naked on the cross is another facet that must be left to speculation. It seems that this was the Roman custom, despite the usual representation on crucifixes of a loincloth of some type. If so, this would certainly add another layer of shame and degradation which we usually pass over. It might have some special significance to our modern world.

It has been said by too many spiritual writers to pass by in silence, that meditation on the Passion and Death of Christ always helps us to manage our own crosses and duties more easily. That's been my experience, too.

Short of actually making a pilgrimage to the Holy Land, the Stations of the Cross and the five Sorrowful Mysteries of the Rosary are powerful devotions to the Passion and Death of Christ. They certainly make the Paschal Mystery, the central act of our salvation, come alive for each one, personally.

And for those who have made the pilgrimage and walked along the Via Dolorosa, these devotions bring back vivid memories that help us relive those sacred events.

* * * * * * * o * * * * * * o * * * * * * *

X.

Fifth Sorrowful Mystery
THE CRUCIFIXION

1. SCRIPTURE

When they had crucified him, they divided his clothes among them by casting lots; then they sat down there and kept watch over him. Above his head they had put the charge against him in writing: "THIS IS JESUS, KING OF THE JEWS."

Two insurgents were crucified along with him, one at his right and one at his left. People going by kept insulting him, tossing their heads and saying: "So you are the one who was going to destroy the temple and rebuild it in three days! Save yourself, why don't you? Come down off that cross if you are God's Son!"

The chief priests, the scribes, and the elders also joined in the jeering: "He saved others but he cannot save himself! So he is the king of Israel! Let's see him come down from that cross and then we will believe in him. He relied on God; let God rescue him now if he wants to. After all, he claimed, 'I am God's Son.' " The insurgents who had been crucified with him kept taunting him in the same way.

From noon onward, there was darkness over the whole land until midafternoon. Then toward midafternoon Jesus cried out in a loud tone, *"Eli, Eli, lema sabachthani?"*, that is, "My God, my God, why have you forsaken me?" This made some of the bystanders who heard it remark, "He is invoking Elijah!"

Immediately one of them ran off and got a sponge. He soaked it in cheap wine, and sticking it on a reed, tried to make him drink. Meanwhile, the rest said, "Leave him alone. Let's see whether Elijah comes to his rescue."

Once again Jesus cried out in a loud voice, and then gave up his spirit.

Suddenly the curtain of the sanctuary was torn in two from top to bottom. The earth quaked, boulders split, tombs opened. Many bodies of saints who had fallen asleep were raised. After Jesus' resurrection they came forth from their tombs and entered the holy city and appeared to many.

The centurion and his men who were keeping watch over Jesus were terror-stricken at seeing the earthquake and all that was happening, and said, "Clearly this was the Son of God!"   Matthew 27:35-54   (NAB)

Then they crucified him and divided up his garments by rolling dice for them to see what each should take. It was about nine in the morning when they crucified him. The inscription proclaiming his offense read, "THE KING OF THE JEWS."

With him they crucified two insurgents, one at his right and one at his left. People going by kept insulting him, tossing their heads and saying, "Ha, ha! So you were going to destroy the temple and rebuild it in three days! Save yourself now by coming down from the cross!"

The chief priests and the scribes also joined in and jeered: "He saved others but he cannot save himself! Let the

'Messiah,' the 'king of Israel,' come down from the cross here and now so that we can see it and believe in him!" The men who had been crucified with him likewise kept taunting him.

When noon came, darkness fell on the whole countryside and lasted until about midafternoon. At that time Jesus cried in a loud voice, *"Eloi, Eloi, lama sabachthani?"* which means, "My God, my God, why have you forsaken me?" A few of the bystanders who heard it remarked, "Listen! He is calling on Elijah!"

Someone ran off, and soaking a sponge in sour wine, stuck it on a reed to try to make him drink. The man said, "Now let's see whether Elijah comes to take him down."

Then Jesus, uttering a loud cry, breathed his last. At that moment the curtain in the sanctuary was torn in two from top to bottom. The centurion who stood guard over him, on seeing the manner of his death, declared, "Clearly this man was the Son of God!"   Mark 15:24-39 (NAB)

Two others who were criminals were led along with him to be crucified. When they came to Skull Place, as it was called, they crucified him there and the criminals as well, one on his right and the other on his left. Jesus said, "Father, forgive them; they do not know what they are doing." They divided his garments, rolling dice for them.

The people stood there watching, and the leaders kept jeering at him saying, "He saved others; let him save himself if he is the Messiah of God, the chosen one." The soldiers also made fun of him, coming forward to offer him their sour wine and saying, "If you are the king of the Jews, save yourself." There was an inscription over his head: "THIS IS THE KING OF THE JEWS."

One of the criminals hanging in crucifixion blasphemed him: "Aren't you the Messiah? Then save yourself and us." But the other one rebuked him: "Have you no fear of God, seeing you are under the same sentence? We deserve it, after all. We are only paying the price for what we've done, but this man has done nothing wrong." He then said, "Jesus, remember me when you enter upon your reign." And Jesus replied, "I assure you: this day you will be with me in paradise."

It was now around midday, and darkness came over the whole land until midafternoon with an eclipse of the sun. The curtain in the sanctuary was torn in two. Jesus uttered a loud cry and said, "Father, into your hands I commend my spirit." After he said this, he expired.

The centurion, upon seeing what had happened, gave glory to God by saying, "Surely this was an innocent man." When the crowd which had assembled for this spectacle saw what had happened, they went home beating their breasts.   Luke 23:32-48   (NAB)

Jesus was led away, and carrying the cross by himself, went out to what is called the Place of the Skull (in Hebrew, *Golgotha*). There they crucified him, and two others with him; one on either side, Jesus in the middle.

Pilate had an inscription placed on the cross which read, JESUS THE NAZOREAN, THE KING OF THE JEWS. This inscription, in Hebrew, Latin, and Greek, was read by many of the Jews, since the place where Jesus was crucified was near the city. The chief priests of the Jews tried to tell Pilate, "You should not have written, 'The King of the Jews.' Write instead, 'This man claimed to be King of the Jews.' " Pilate answered, "What I have written, I have written."

After the soldiers had crucified Jesus, they took his garments and divided them four ways, one for each soldier. There was also his tunic, but this tunic was woven in one piece from top to bottom and had no seam. They said to each other, "We should not tear it. Let us throw dice to see who gets it." (The purpose of this was to have the Scripture fulfilled: "They divided my garments among them; for my clothing they cast lots.") And this was what the soldiers did.

Near the cross of Jesus there stood his mother, his mother's sister, Mary the wife of Clopas, and Mary Magdalene. Seeing his mother there with the disciple whom he loved, Jesus said to his mother, "Woman, there is your son." In turn he said to the disciple, "There is your mother." From that hour onward, the disciple took her into his care.

After that, Jesus, realizing that everything was now finished, said to fulfill the Scripture, "I am thirsty." There was a jar there, full of common wine. They stuck a sponge soaked in this wine on some hyssop and raised it to his lips. When Jesus took the wine, he said, "Now it is finished." Then he bowed his head, and delivered over his spirit.

Since it was the Preparation Day, the Jews did not want to have the bodies left on the cross during the sabbath, for that sabbath was a solemn feast day. They asked Pilate that the legs be broken and the bodies be taken away. Accordingly, the soldiers came and broke the legs of the men crucified with Jesus, first the one, then the other.

When they came to Jesus and saw that he was already dead, they did not break his legs. One of the soldiers thrust a lance into his side, and immediately blood and water flowed out. (This testimony has been given by an eyewitness, and his testimony is true. He tells what he knows is true, so that you may believe.)

These events took place for the fulfillment of Scripture: "Break none of his bones." There is still another Scripture passage which says: "They shall look on him whom they have pierced."   John 19:16-37   (NAB)

My God, my God, why have you forsaken me, far from my prayer, from the words of my cry? . . .

All who see me scoff at me; they mock me with parted lips, they wag their heads:

"He relied on the Lord, let him deliver him, let him rescue him if he loves him." . . .

They divide my garments among them, and for my vesture they cast lots.   Psalm 22:2, 8-9, 19   (NAB)

[The paschal lamb] You shall not break any of its bones.   Exodus 12:46   (NAB)

I will pour out on the house of David and on the inhabitants of Jerusalem a spirit of grace and petition; and they shall look on him whom they have thrust through, and they shall mourn for him as one mourns for an only son, and they shall grieve over him as one grieves over a first-born.   Zechariah 12:10   (NAB)

2. ANCIENT AUTHORS

St. John Chrysostom: *Homilies on John*, #85

And so He was crucified, and with Him thieves, unwittingly fulfilling prophecy in this detail also. Indeed, the very things which were done to revile Him were the ones that contributed to reveal the truth, in order that you might learn its power. I say this for the prophet had foretold this circumstance also, from ancient times in the words, "He was reputed with the wicked."

And Pilate also wrote an inscription — at the same time to avenge himself, and even to defend Christ. Pilate set the inscription in place as if it were to serve as a kind of trophy, giving voice to a splendid message. Moreover, he made this clear, not in one tongue only, but in three languages. He did this because Christ was slandered even when He was on the cross.

Now, the soldiers divided His garments among themselves, but not His tunic. Notice how they frequently caused prophecies to be fulfilled by their wicked deeds, for this deed had also been foretold. Kindly notice the exactness of the prophecy, too. The prophet declared not only that they divided the garments among themselves, but also that they did not rend them. Thus, the soldiers divided some of Christ's garments into parts, but they did not divide the tunic; on the contrary, they settled its possession by lot.

He himself, though crucified, gave His Mother to His disciple's keeping to instruct us to take care of our parents, even to our last breath. Here, Christ showed great tenderness and gave Mary into the keeping of the disciple whom He loved. Why did He address no other word to John and give him no comfort in his grief? Because it was not the time for words of consolation. Besides, he received the reward for his fidelity in that he was deemed worthy of such an honor as this.

Notice, also, how He did everything with calmness, even though crucified: speaking to the disciple about His Mother, fulfilling prophecies, holding out to the thief fair hope for the future. Yet, before being crucified He was observed to be sweating, in an agony, fearful. Why was this? In the previous time, the frailty of His human nature was demonstrated, while here the infinite extent of His power was being shown.

St. Hilary of Poitiers: *The Trinity*, Bk. 3

The Son clearly glorifies the Father because He says, "I have glorified You on earth, since I have accomplished the work that you have given me to do." The praise of the Father comes completely from the Son, because those things for which the Son will be acclaimed will be a commendation of the Father. He fulfills everything that the Father has willed.

The Son of God is born as a man, but the power of God is manifested at His birth from the Virgin. The Son of God is seen as a man, but appears as God in the works of man. The Son of God is nailed to the cross, but on the cross God overcomes the death of man.

Christ, the Son of God, dies, but all flesh is vivified in Christ. The more such things are praised in Christ, the greater will be the approbation of Him from whom Christ as God derives his origin. By such means as these, therefore, does the Father glorify the Son on earth, and again, the Son by the miracles of His power gives glory to Him from Whom He comes in the sight of the ignorant and foolish world.

Therefore, the Father has been glorified by the miracles of the Son when He is recognized as God, when He is revealed as the Father of the only-begotten, when for our salvation He even willed that His Son be born as man from the Virgin, and in Him all those things, which began with the birth from the Virgin, are accomplished in the Passion.

3. Recent Authors

St. Robert Bellarmine: *Homily on the Seven Words*

The task that Our Lord gave to St. John of caring for the Virgin Mother was certainly a light burden and a sweet yoke. Who would not joyfully take into his own home the Mother in whose womb the Word lived for nine months, and under whose loving care He lived for thirty years?

Who would not envy this beloved disciple of the Lord who, when His Lord was gone, was granted the presence of the Mother? And yet, I feel that we, too, may have her presence granted by our prayers. The most merciful Lord, Who was born for us, and, in His great love, crucified for us, will respond and say to each of us, "Behold, your Mother"; and to her, "Behold, each one of these, your sons and daughters."

Nor will this most loving Virgin hesitate to embrace in her maternal love so great a multitude of children. She ardently desires that not a single soul perish whom her Son has redeemed by His precious Blood in His saving death.

St. Thomas More: *Prison Letter*

By the merits of His bitter passion joined to mine and far surpassing in merit for me all that I can suffer myself, His bounteous goodness shall release me from the pains of purgatory and shall increase my reward in heaven besides.

Vatican II: *Sacrosanctum Concilium*, #5

The work of man's redemption of God's perfect glory was foreshadowed by God's mighty deeds among the people of the Old Covenant. It was brought to fulfillment by Christ the Lord, especially through the paschal mystery of His blessed passion, resurrection from the dead and ascension into glory.

By dying He destroyed our death, by rising He restored our life. . . .

M.W. Schoenberg: *Crucifixion* (edited)

Crucifixion was a method of capital punishment in common use among the ancient peoples who lived around the Mediterranean from about the sixth century B.C. until abolished by Constantine the Great, the first Catholic Emperor in 338 A.D. as a token of respect for Christ.

Because of its extreme cruelty, crucifixion was intended both as a severe punishment and as a deterrent to crime, a frightful deterrent. It was intended to be a lengthy, excruciatingly slow way of death. The first mention of impalement actually is found in the Code of Hammurabi in the seventeenth century B.C.

It was never practiced in Greece, and was foreign to Jewish law. But the Romans eventually used it as a common practice whenever the occasion seemed to warrant it. They considered it so shameful that Roman citizens were routinely exempted from it.

The victim was always scourged, first, then driven naked through the street, carrying the crossbeam on his shoulders, to the place of execution, where the upright support was already implanted in the ground. To prolong the agony a support was given to the body by a back support, and by binding or nailing the feet.

Death could later be hastened by breaking the legs or piercing the body with a spear. After the death, the body was left to rot on the cross.

Jesus suffered a true crucifixion as recorded in the gospels. The body was taken down after death in accordance with Jewish custom of burying on the day of death. Because of the Jewish feelings against nudity, he was probably not nude on the cross.

Negro Spiritual: *Were You There?*

> Were you there when they crucified my Lord?
> Were you there when they crucified my Lord?
> Oh! . . . Sometimes it causes me to tremble, tremble,
>   tremble.
> Were you there when they crucified my Lord?

Were you there when they nailed Him to the tree?
Were you there when they nailed Him to the tree?
Oh! . . . sometimes it causes me to tremble, tremble,
    tremble.
Were you there when they nailed Him to the tree?

Were you there when they laid Him in the tomb?
Were you there when they laid Him in the tomb?
Oh! . . . sometimes it causes me to tremble, tremble,
    tremble.
Were you there when they laid Him in the tomb?

Were you there when they rolled the stone away?
Were you there when they rolled the stone away?
Oh! . . . sometimes it causes me to tremble, tremble,
    tremble.
Were you there when they rolled the stone away?

4. MEDITATION

It's almost impossible to add anything to the gospel accounts of the crucifixion. Yes, we can check the encyclopedias, the histories and the biblical scholars to get even more details of what a Roman crucifixion was like, and it's pretty horrifying.

The Italian and Spanish saints were very graphic in their sermons about the death of Christ and many of their artists depict the event in all its gruesome detail. The pounding of the nails, the wrenchings of the body, the shock of the erection of the cross, and so on.

The Fathers liked to dwell on the theological depths of this event and to show it for the great work of our redemption that it is. They see the glory of God and His mercy and love for a fallen race that could do nothing to save itself until the Son came, Incarnate. How majestic was their understanding.

Somehow St. Thomas More's calm, assured faith in the merits Christ won on Calvary, and the stark questions of the Negro Spiritual say more to me than all the dramatics of the impassioned preacher.

Let the gospel accounts speak for themselves. Let them touch your soul.

PART THREE

THE
GLORIOUS MYSTERIES

* * * * *   ○   * * * * * * *   ○   * * * * *

* * * * * * o * * * * * * o * * * * * *

XI.
First Glorious Mystery:
THE RESURRECTION

1. SCRIPTURE

After the sabbath, as the first day of the week was dawning, Mary Magdalene came with the other Mary to inspect the tomb. Suddenly there was a mighty earthquake as the angel of the Lord descended from heaven. He came to the stone, rolled it back and sat on it. In appearance he resembled a flash of lightning while his garments were as dazzling as snow.

The guards grew paralyzed with fear of him and fell down like dead men. Then the angel spoke, addressing the women:

"Do not be frightened. I know you are looking for Jesus the crucified, but he is not here. He has been raised, exactly as he promised. Come and see the place where he was laid. Then go quickly and tell his disciples: 'He has been raised from the dead and now goes ahead of you to Galilee, where you will see him.' That is the message I have for you."

They hurried away from the tomb half-overjoyed, half-fearful, and ran to carry the good news to his disciples.

Suddenly, without warning, Jesus stood before them and said, "Peace!" The women came up and embraced his feet and did him homage.

At this Jesus said to them, "Do not be afraid! Go and carry the news to my brothers that they are to go to Galilee, where they will see me."

As the women were returning, some of the guards went into the city and reported to the chief priests all that had happened. They in turn, convened with the elders and worked out their strategy, giving the soldiers a large bribe with the instructions: "You are to say, 'His disciples came during the night and stole him while we were asleep.' If any word of this gets to the procurator, we will straighten it out with him and keep you out of trouble."

The soldiers pocketed the money and did as they had been instructed. This is the story that circulates among the Jews to this very day.

The eleven disciples made their way to Galilee, to the mountain to which Jesus had summoned them. At the sight of him, those who had entertained doubts fell down in homage. Jesus came forward and addressed them in these words:

"Full authority has been given to me both in heaven and on earth; go, therefore, and make disciples of all the nations. Baptize them in the name of the Father, and of the Son and of the Holy Spirit.

"Teach them to carry out everything I have commanded you. And know that I am with you always, until the end of the world."   Matthew Ch. 28   (NAB)

When the Sabbath was over, Mary Magdalene, Mary the mother of James, and Salome bought perfumed oils with which they intended to go and anoint Jesus. Very early, just after sunrise, on the first day of the week they came to the tomb. They were saying to one another, "Who will roll back the stone for us from the entrance to the tomb?"

When they looked, they found that the stone had been rolled back. (It was a huge one.) On entering the tomb they saw a young man sitting at the right, dressed in a white robe. This frightened them thoroughly, but he reassured them:

"You need not be amazed! You are looking for Jesus of Nazareth, the one who was crucified. He has been raised up; he is not here. See the place where they laid him. Go now and tell his disciples and Peter, 'He is going ahead of you to Galilee, where you will see him just as he told you.'"

They made their way out and fled from the tomb bewildered and trembling; and because of their great fear, they said nothing to anyone.

Jesus rose from the dead early on the first day of the week. He first appeared to Mary Magdalene, out of whom he had cast seven demons. She went to announce the good news to his followers, who were now grieving and weeping. But when they heard that he was alive and had been seen by her, they refused to believe it.

Later on, as two of them were walking along on their way to the country, he was revealed to them completely changed in appearance. These men retraced their steps and announced the good news to the others; but the others put no more faith in them than in Mary Magdalene.

Finally, as they were at table, Jesus was revealed to the eleven. He took them to task for their disbelief and their stubbornness, since they had put no faith in those who had seen him after he had been raised.

Then he told them: "Go into the whole world and proclaim the good news to all creation. The man who believes in it and accepts baptism will be saved; the man who refuses to believe in it will be condemned. Signs like these will accompany those who have professed their faith: they will use my name to expel demons, they will speak entirely new languages, they will be able to handle serpents, they will be able to drink deadly poison without harm, and the sick upon whom they lay their hands will recover."

Mark 16:1-18   (NAB)

On the first day of the week, at dawn, the women came to the tomb bringing the spices they had prepared. They found the stone rolled back from the tomb; but when they entered the tomb, they did not find the body of the Lord Jesus.

While they were still at a loss over what to think of this, two men in dazzling garments stood beside them. Terrified, the women bowed to the ground. The men said to them: "Why do you search for the Living One among the dead? He is not here; he has been raised up. Remember what he said to you while he was still in Galilee — that the Son of Man must be delivered into the hands of sinful men, and be crucified, and on the third day rise again." With this reminder, his words came back to them.

On their return from the tomb, they told all these things to the Eleven and the others. The women were Mary of Magdala, Joanna, and Mary the mother of James. The older women with them also told the apostles, but the story seemed like nonsense and they refused to believe them. Peter, however, got up and ran to the tomb. He stooped down but could see nothing but the wrappings. So he went away full of amazement at what had occurred.

Two of them that same day were making their way to a village named Emmaus seven miles distant from Jerusalem, discussing as they went all that had happened. In the course of their lively exchange, Jesus approached and began to walk along with them. However, they were restrained from recognizing him.

He said to them, "What are you discussing as you go your way?" They halted, in distress, and one of them, Cleopas by name, asked him, "Are you the only resident of Jerusalem who does not know the things that went on there these past few days?" He said to them, "What things?"

They said: "All those that had to do with Jesus of Nazareth, a prophet powerful in word and deed in the eyes of God and the people; how our chief priests and leaders delivered him up to be condemned to death, and crucified him. We were hoping that he was the one who would set Israel free.

"Besides all this, today, the third day since these things happened, some women of our group have just brought us some astonishing news. They were at the tomb before dawn and failed to find his body, but returned with the tale that they had seen a vision of angels who declared he was alive. Some of our number went to the tomb and found it to be just as the women said, but him they did not see."

Then he said to them, "What little sense you have! How slow you are to believe all that the prophets have announced! Did not the Messiah have to undergo all this so as to enter his glory?" Beginning, then, with Moses and all the prophets, he interpreted for them every passage of Scripture which referred to him.

By now they were near the village to which they were going, and he acted as if he were going farther. But they pressed him: "Stay with us. It is nearly evening — the day is practically over." So he went in to stay with them.

When he had seated himself with them to eat, he took bread, pronounced the blessing, then broke the bread and began to distribute it to them. With that their eyes were opened and they recognized him; whereupon he vanished from their sight. They said to one another, "Were not our hearts burning inside us as he talked to us on the road and explained the Scriptures to us?"

They got up immediately and returned to Jerusalem, where they found the Eleven and the rest of the company assembled. They were greeted with. "The Lord has been raised! It is true! He has appeared to Simon." Then they recounted what had happened on the road and how they had come to know him in the breaking of the bread.

While they were still speaking about all this, he himself stood in their midst and said to them, "Peace to you." In their panic and fright they thought they were seeing a ghost.

He said to them, "Why are you disturbed? Why do such ideas cross your mind? Look at my hands and my feet; it is really I. Touch me, and see that a ghost does not have flesh and bones as I do."

As he said this he showed them his hands and his feet. They were still incredulous for sheer joy and wonder, so he said to them, "Have you something here to eat?" They gave him a piece of cooked fish, which he took and ate in their presence.

Then he said to them, "Recall those words I spoke to you when I was still with you; everything written about me in the law of Moses and the prophets and psalms had to be fulfilled." Then he opened their minds to the understanding of the Scriptures.

He said to them: "Thus it is written that the Messiah must suffer and rise from the dead on the third day. In his name, penance for the remission of sins is to be preached to all the nations, beginning at Jerusalem. You are witnesses of this. See, I send down upon you the promise of my Father. Remain here in the city until you are clothed with power from on high."   Luke 24:1-49   (NAB)

Early in the morning on the first day of the week, while it was still dark, Mary Magdalene came to the tomb. She saw that the stone had been moved away, so she ran off to Simon Peter and the other disciple (the one Jesus loved) and told them, "The Lord has been taken from the tomb! We don't know where they have put him!"

At that, Peter and the other disciple started out on their way toward the tomb. They were running side by side, but then the other disciple outran Peter and reached the tomb first. He did not enter but bent down to peer in, and saw the wrappings lying on the ground.

Presently, Simon Peter came along behind him and entered the tomb. He observed the wrappings on the ground and saw the piece of cloth which had covered the head not lying with the wrappings, but rolled up in a place by itself.

Then the disciple who had arrived first at the tomb went in. He saw and believed. (Remember, as yet they did not understand the Scripture that Jesus had to rise from the dead.) With this, the disciples went back home.

Meanwhile, Mary stood weeping beside the tomb. Even as she wept, she stooped to peer inside, and there she saw two angels in dazzling robes. One was seated at the head and the other at the foot of the place where Jesus' body had lain. "Woman," they asked her, "why are you weeping?" She answered them, "Because the Lord has been taken away, and I do not know where they have put him."

She had no sooner said this than she turned around and caught sight of Jesus standing there. But she did not know him. "Woman," he asked her, "why are you weeping?" She supposed he was the gardener, so she said, "Sir, if you are the one who carried him off, tell me where you have laid him and I will take him away."

Jesus said to her, "Mary!" She turned to him and said in Hebrew, "*Rabbouni!*" (meaning "Teacher"). Jesus then said: "Do not cling to me, for I have not yet ascended to the Father. Rather, go to my brothers and tell them, 'I am ascending to my Father and your Father, to my God and your God!'" Mary Magdalene went to the disciples. "I have seen the Lord!" she announced. Then she reported what he had said to her.

On the evening of that first day of the week, even though the disciples had locked the doors of the place where they were for fear of the Jews, Jesus came and stood before them. "Peace be with you," he said. When he said this, he showed them his hands and his side. At the sight of the Lord the disciples rejoiced. "Peace be with you," he said again. "As the Father has sent me, so I send you." Then he breathed on them and said: "Receive the Holy Spirit. If you forgive men's sins, they are forgiven them; if you hold them bound, they are held bound."

It happened that one of the Twelve, Thomas (the name means "Twin") was absent when Jesus came. The other disciples kept telling him: "We have seen the Lord!" His answer was, "I will never believe it without probing the nailprints in his hands, without putting my finger in the nailmarks and my hand into his side."

A week later, the disciples were once more in the room, and this time Thomas was with them. Despite the locked doors, Jesus came and stood before them. "Peace be with you," he said; then, to Thomas: "Take your finger and examine my hands. Put your hand into my side. Do not persist in your unbelief, but believe!" Thomas said in response, "My Lord and my God!" Jesus then said to him: "You became a believer because you saw me. Blest are they who have not seen and have believed."

Jesus performed many other signs as well — signs not recorded here — in the presence of his disciples. But these have been recorded to help you believe that Jesus is the Messiah, the Son of God, so that through this faith you may have life in his name. . . . There are still many other things that Jesus did, yet if they were written about in detail, I doubt there would be room enough in the entire world to hold the books to record them.

John 20:1-31; 21:25   (NAB)

[Peter then said:] "Men of Israel, listen to me! Jesus the Nazorean was a man whom God sent to you with miracles, wonders, and signs as his credentials. These God worked through him in your midst, as you well know. He was delivered up by the set purpose and plan of God; you even made use of pagans to crucify and kill him. God freed him from death's bitter pangs, however, and raised him up again, for it was impossible that death should keep its hold on him." Acts 2:22-24   (NAB)

Brothers, I want to remind you of the gospel I preached to you, which you received and in which you stand firm. You are being saved by it at this very moment if you hold fast to it as I preached it to you. Otherwise you have believed in vain.

I handed on to you first of all what I myself received, that Christ died for our sins in accordance with the Scriptures; that he was buried and, in accordance with the Scriptures, rose on the third day; that he was seen by Cephas, then by the Twelve. After that he was seen by five hundred brothers at once, most of whom are still alive, although some have fallen asleep. Next he was seen by James; then by all the apostles.

Last of all he was seen by me, as one born out of the normal course. I am the least of the apostles; in fact, because I persecuted the church of God, I do not even deserve the name. But by God's favor I am what I am. This favor of his to me has not proved fruitless. Indeed, I have worked harder than all the others, not on my own but through the favor of God. In any case, whether it be I or they, this is what we preach and this is what you believed.

Tell me, if Christ is preached as raised from the dead, how is it that some of you say there is no resurrection from the dead? If there is no resurrection of the dead, Christ himself has not been raised. And if Christ has not been raised, our preaching is void of content and your faith is empty too.

Indeed, we should then be exposed as false witnesses of God, for we have borne witness before him that he raised up Christ; but he certainly did not raise him up if the dead are not raised. Why? Because if the dead are not raised, then Christ was not raised; and if Christ was not raised, your faith is worthless. You are still in your sins, and those who have fallen asleep in Christ are the deadest of the dead. If our hopes in Christ are limited to this life only, we are the most pitiable of men.

But as it is, Christ is now raised from the dead, the first fruits of those who have fallen asleep.

                                  1 Corinthians 15:1-20   (NAB)

2. Ancient Authors

St. Peter Chrysologus: *Sermon 74 on Christ's Resurrection*

Today we shall consider the Lord's Resurrection. In relation to this, if Christ's birth from the Virgin is something divine, how much more so is His Resurrection from the dead! Therefore, let not that which is divine be heard with merely human interpretation.

"Late in the night of the Sabbath," Scripture says, "as it began to dawn towards the first day of the week." The evening of the Sabbath — for the world, evening terminates the day; it does not begin it. The evening fades into darkness; it does not grow bright. It does not change into dawn because it does not know the sunrise.

Evening, the mother of night, gives birth to daylight! It changes the customary order while it acknowledges its Creator. It displays a new symbolic mystery. It is eager to serve its Creator rather than the march of time.

"Late in the night of the Sabbath," we read, "as it began to dawn towards the first day of the week, Mary Magdalene and the other Mary came to see the sepulchre." Earlier a woman hastened to sin; now, later on, a woman hastens to repentance. In the morning a woman knew that she had corrupted Adam; in the evening a woman seeks Christ.

"Mary Magdalene and the other Mary came to see the sepulchre." A woman had drawn a beginning of perfidy out of paradise; now a woman hastens to draw faith from the sepulchre. She who had snatched death out of life now hurries to get life out of death.

"Mary came." This is the name of Christ's mother. Therefore, the one who hastened was a mother in name. She came as a woman, that woman who had become the mother of those who die, might become the mother of the living, and fulfillment might be had in the Scriptural statement about her: "that is, the mother of all the living."

"Mary came to the sepulchre." The sight of the tree had deceived her; the sight of the sepulchre was to restore her. A guileful glance had laid her low; a saving glance was to raise her up again.

"And behold," the Gospel continues, "there was a great earthquake; for an angel of the Lord came down from heaven." The earth trembled, not because an angel came down from heaven, but because its Ruler ascended from hell. Hell is caught and set in its place. Death gets judged — death which, rushing against guilty men, runs into its Judge; death which after long domination over its slaves rose up against its Master; death which waxed fierce against men but encountered God.

The power of death was taken away, and in penalty for its rashness in attempting to harm its Judge, death brought the dead back to life. Bodies were yielded up. The Man was put back together, and His life was restored, and now everything holds together through forgiveness, because the condemnation has passed over on to the Author of life.

Through the Resurrection of Christ and the defeat of death, men once more entered into relationship with heaven.

"For an angel of the Lord came down from heaven and drawing near rolled back the stone and sat upon it." Rolled back the stone — when rolled forward it was the sign of his death; rolled back it is the symbol of His Resurrection. And the angel sat as a sign that he was a teacher of the faith and the doctor of the Resurrection. The angel was placing the foundations of faith upon the rock, in which Christ built His Church, as He said, "You are Peter, and upon this rock I will build my Church."

"His countenance was like lightning," the Gospel says, "and his raiment like snow." Is not brilliance of lightning enough for an angel? What did raiment add to heavenly nature? But by such splendor he foreshadowed the beauty and the pattern of our resurrection. For those who arise in Christ are transformed with the glory of Christ.

Melito of Sardis: *Homily on Easter*

Understand, that the paschal mystery is, at the same time, both old and new, transitory and eternal, corruptible and incorruptible, mortal and immortal. In terms of the Law it is old, in terms of the Word it is new. In its figure it is passing, in its grace it is eternal. It is corruptible in the sacrifice of the lamb, incorruptible in the eternal life of the Lord. It is mortal in his burial, immortal in his resurrection from the dead.

The Law indeed is old, but the Word is new. The type is transitory, the grace is eternal. The Lamb was corruptible, but the Lord is incorruptible. He was slain as a lamb; he rose again as God. He was silent as a lamb, yet he was not a lamb.

The type has passed away; the reality has come. The lamb gives place to God, the sheep gives place to a man, and the man is Christ, who fills the whole of creation. The sacrifice of the lamb, the celebration of Passover and the prescriptions of the Law have been fulfilled in Jesus Christ. Under the old Law, and still more under the new dispensation, everything pointed toward him.

Both the Law and the Word came forth from Zion and Jerusalem, but now the Law has given place to the Word, the old to the new. The commandment has become grace, the type a reality. The lamb has become a Son, the sheep a man, and man, God.

The Lord, though he was God, became man, He suffered for the sake of those who suffer, he was bound for those in bonds, condemned for the guilty, buried for those who lie in disgrace; but he rose from the dead, and cried aloud: "Who will contend with me? Let him confront me!"

Come, then, O Gentiles, receive forgiveness for the sins that defile you. I am your forgiveness. I am the Passover that

brings salvation. I am the lamb who was immolated for you.
I am your ransom, your life, your resurrection, your light; I
am your salvation and your king. I will bring you to the
heights of heaven. With my right hand I will raise you up,
and I will show you the eternal Father: I am Christ.

3. RECENT AUTHORS

Pheme Perkins: *Resurrection*

Many people would immediately think of the stories of
Jesus' empty tomb as the central content of Christian
preaching about Easter. Yet our oldest examples of an early
Christian witness to Resurrection, the formula that Paul
reports in 1 Corinthians 15:3-5, does not say anything about
the tomb.

Instead we find a tradition that focuses on the experience of having seen the Lord. Finding a person's tomb
empty would not, in itself, have led to the conclusion that the
person had been raised, since resurrection was associated
with the imagery of final judgment and the end of the world.

However, the combination of an early tradition of ap-
pearances of the Lord and the conviction that Jesus' tomb
was empty would help explain the significance of resurrection in the Christian message about Jesus.

Father Xavier Leon-Dufour, S.J.: *Resurrection and the Message of Easter*

When the disciples from Emmaus rejoined the Eleven
in Jerusalem and told them the news of their meeting with
Christ, the reply they received was, "The Lord has risen
indeed and has appeared to Simon" (Luke 24:34). In all

likelihood this became a traditional formula in the early Christian community.

Similarly, Paul in his first letter to the Corinthians quotes a formula the character of which is clearly derived from liturgy and tradition. "I delivered to you as of first importance what I also received, that Christ died for our sins in accordance with the scriptures, that he was buried. That he was raised on the third day in accordance with the scriptures."

Here, Paul reminds his brethren in the faith of the Good News in which they have believed and by which they will be saved, the Word which Paul had received and handed on in his turn as the living core of the faith (1 Corinthians 15:11). It is no concern of Paul's to prove that Jesus had risen, but only to reason from a common basis of faith.

4. MEDITATION

St. Augustine reminds us that Christians are an Easter people and "Alleluia is our song." We sing in the Liturgy of Easter Week, "This is the day the Lord has made, let us rejoice and be glad in it." And in daily Mass we often pray, "Christ has died, Christ is risen, Christ will come again."

Faith in the risen Christ is a living part of contemporary Christian living. Each age has made this faith especially its own with an emphasis on some aspects of it over and above others. But the common theme that unites them all is the joy of the Resurrection that means a shared new life.

Christ alive, Christ who can never die again, Christ triumphant shares that life with us, through Baptism and the other sacraments. But Baptism is the real "Easter Sacrament." We are called to eternal life, life guaranteed by the fact of Christ, risen and alive.

The Rite for the Christian Initiation of Adults (RCIA) has restored the emphasis on Baptism in the Easter Vigil liturgy. It demonstrates that the hope in the Easter event still attracts men and women.

* * * * * * * ○ * * * * * * * ○ * * * * * * *

XII.
Second Glorious Mystery
THE ASCENSION

1. SCRIPTURE

The eleven disciples made their way to Galilee, to the mountain to which Jesus had summoned them. At the sight of him, those who had entertained doubts fell down in homage. Jesus came forward and addressed them in these words:

> "Full authority has been given to me both in heaven
>   and on earth;
>
> go, therefore, and make disciples of all the nations.
>
> Baptize them in the name
>   of the Father,
>   and of the Son,
>   and of the Holy Spirit.
>
> Teach them to carry out everything I have
>   commanded you.
>
> And know that I am with you always,
>   until the end of the world!"
>
> Matthew 28:16-20   (NAB)

Then, after speaking to them, the Lord Jesus was taken up into heaven and took his seat at God's right hand. The Eleven went forth and preached everywhere. The Lord continued to work with them throughout and confirmed the message through the signs which accompanied them.

Mark 16:19-20   (NAB)

Then he led them out near Bethany, and with hands upraised, blessed them. As he blessed, he left them, and was taken up to heaven. They fell down to do him reverence, then returned to Jerusalem filled with joy. There they were to be found in the temple constantly, speaking the praises of God.   Luke 24:50-53   (NAB)

In my first account, Theophilus, I dealt with all that Jesus did and taught until the day he was taken up to heaven, having first instructed the apostles he had chosen through the Holy Spirit. In the time after his suffering he showed them in many convincing ways that he was alive, appearing to them over the course of forty days and speaking to them about the reign of God.

On one occasion when he met with them, he told them not to leave Jerusalem: "Wait, rather, for the fulfillment of my Father's promise, of which you have heard me speak. John baptized with water, but within a few days you will be baptized with the Holy Spirit."

While they were with him they asked, "Lord, are you going to restore the rule to Israel now?" His answer was: "The exact time is not yours to know. The Father has reserved that to Himself. You will receive power when the Holy Spirit comes down on you; then you are to be my witnesses in Jerusalem, throughout Judea and Samaria, yes, even to the ends of the earth."

No sooner had he said this than he was lifted up before their eyes in a cloud which took him from their sight.

They were still gazing up into the heavens when two men dressed in white stood beside them. "Men of Galilee," they said, "why do you stand here looking up at the skies? This Jesus who has been taken from you will return, just as you saw him go up into the heavens."

After that they returned to Jerusalem from the mount called Olivet near Jerusalem — a mere sabbath's journey away. Entering the city, they went to the upstairs room where they were staying: Peter and John and James and Andrew; Philip and Thomas, Bartholomew and Matthew; James son of Alpheus; Simon, the Zealot party member, and Judas son of James. Together they devoted themselves to constant prayer. There were some women in their company, and Mary the mother of Jesus, and his brothers.

Acts 1:1-14   (NAB)

Each of us has received God's favor in the measure in which Christ bestows it. Thus you find Scripture saying:

"When he ascended on high, he took a host of captives and gave gifts to men."

"He ascended" — what does this mean but that he had first descended into the lower regions of the earth? He who descended is the very one who ascended high above the heavens, that he might fill all men with his gifts.

Ephesians 4:7-10   (NAB)

You have ascended on high, taken captives.
received men as gifts —
even rebels; the Lord God enters his dwelling.

Psalm 68:19   (NAB)

He went to heaven and is at God's right hand, with angelic rulers and powers subjected to him.

1 Peter 3:22 (NAB)

2. ANCIENT AUTHORS

St. Augustine: *The City of God*

It seems incredible that Christ should have risen in the flesh, and with His flesh have ascended into heaven; it seems incredible that the world should have believed such a thing; it seems incredible that men so rude and lowly, so few and unaccomplished should have convinced the world, including men of learning, of something so incredible, and have convinced men so conclusively.

It is no less a fact that the Resurrection of Christ and His Ascension into heaven, with the flesh in which He rose, is now preached to the whole world and is believed. Of course, the whole world could believe without a miracle if a multitude of senators, imperial courtiers, and famous scholars had declared that they had seen the Ascension and then took the pains to publicize the fact, but truth is that the world has believed a handful of unknown and unlearned nobodies who said and wrote that they had seen a miracle.

The world has believed this insignificant group of lowly, unimportant and uneducated men precisely because the divine character of what happened is more marvelously apparent in the insignificance of such witnesses. What gave power to the preachers who persuaded the world was not the eloquence of the words they uttered, but the miracles in the deeds they did.

Those who had not themselves seen Christ rising from the dead and ascending into heaven with His flesh believed the men who said they had seen the miracles, not merely because these men said so, but also because these men themselves worked miracles. For example, many people were astonished to hear these men who knew but two languages (and in some cases, only one) suddenly break forth into so many tongues that everybody in the audience understood them [Acts 2:5-6].

They saw a man who had been lame from earliest infancy now, after forty years, stand upright at a word uttered by these witnesses who spoke in the name of Christ [Acts 3:1-10]. Pieces of cloth that touched their bodies were found to heal the sick. Uncounted people suffering from various diseases set themselves in line in the streets where the Apostles passed and where their shadows would fall upon the sick, and many of these people were at once restored to health [Acts 5:6-12].

In such a period how could the possibilities so counter to experience as the Resurrection of Christ's flesh and His Ascension into heaven have found entrance into men's ears and hearts and minds, unless the possibility had been realized in fact, and a proof had been found in the divinity of the fact involved, namely, the fact of the divinity, not to mention the corroboration of manifest miracles? The fact is that, in spite of the terrors and attacks, inspired by a series of fierce persecutions, not only was the Resurrection of Christ loyally believed and fearlessly proclaimed, but also the resurrection and immortality of the bodies of His followers in the world to come.

And the seeds of this hope throughout the world were watered by the blood of martyrs. Not only did men read the earlier prophecies of those future realities, but they saw the miracles that occurred, and were soon convinced that the reality, new as it was to experience, was not counter to reason. The result was that the truth that the world once rejected with all the fury of hate it now sought with the fervor of faith.

Eusebius: *Ecclesiastical History*

At the beginning of the Roman Empire, there appeared to all men and to the Gentiles throughout the world, as if previously assisted and now actually ready for the reception of the knowledge of the Father, the same Teacher of the virtues, the Assistant of the Father in all good things, the divine and heavenly Word of God, in a human body in no way different from the substance of our own nature.

And He performed and suffered such things as were in accord with the prophecies which foretold that One who was both man and God would come to dwell in the world, as the performer of miraculous deeds, and that He would be made manifest to all the Gentiles as the Teacher of the worship of the Father, and that the marvels of His birth and His new teaching and the wonder of His deeds, and, in addition to these, the manner of His death and resurrection from the dead, and above all, His divine Ascension into heaven would also be manifest.

3. RECENT AUTHORS

Frank J. Sheed: *To Know Christ Jesus*

In the Acts, Luke tells us that Jesus was with them for forty days, before he ascended into the sky, and a cloud took him out of their sight. If we had only his Gospel, we might very well think that Jesus ascended on the evening of his resurrection, and we might get the same idea from John (20:17), where, on the morning of his resurrection he tells Mary Magdalene to tell his brethren: "I ascend to my Father and to your Father, to my God and your God."

But Luke in the Acts makes it clear that the rising into the sky, seen by the eleven, took place after forty days; none of which gives us any indication of what other contact there may have been in that period between the Risen Lord and his Father in heaven.

The ascension was from the Mount of Olives. The very last words the apostles said to him were: "Will you at this time restore the kingdom to Israel?" It is the old obsession. They needed the Holy Spirit. And the Holy Spirit did come upon them, as he had promised. Pentecost was ten days after.

Resurrection and ascension are not simply there as a happy ending to a story of suffering and death. Of this the Ordinary of the Mass reminds us: the Mass commemorates not the death only, but the resurrection and the ascension as well. They are essential parts of the sacrifice of our redemption, not a sequel to it.

The sacrifice Jesus offered (1 Cor 5:7; Eph 5:2) was wholly in his humanity, so that it might be applied to the sins of men; but he who offered it was God, so it had a value no purely human sacrifice could have. It was wholly effective in redeeming men from sin.

Father Charles J. Callen, O.P.: *The Acts
of the Apostles*

"You men of Galilee. . . ." All the Apostles, except Judas, were from Galilee. The angels reminded the Apostles that they had a work to perform, and they should be about it. To console them, and to impress upon them the great fact of Christ's coming at the end to judge the world, the angels announce that Our Lord will come again with the same body which has just disappeared, clothed with power and majesty (cf. Luke 21:27).

As it is here stated that the disciples returned from Mt. Olivet, it would appear that the Ascension took place from the highest point on Olivet as tradition has handed down. This was a Sabbath's day journey from Jerusalem — under one mile. Luke, however, says he led them to Bethany, a two-mile walk, farther East. Most likely Our Lord went first to Bethany by the lower road and then ascended the mountain from the East. The two accounts are not opposed.

Father Prospero Grech, O.S.A.: *Acts of the Apostles Explained*

After the last apparition, Jesus ascended into heaven where He was enthroned at the right hand of the Father. There He received that same glory He had before His Incarnation (Jn. 17:5), which had been hidden during His earthly life. God crowned the work of Christ, His humility and His obedience unto death on the Cross, raising Him to the dignity that was His due as the Son of God (Phil. 2:7-11).

In anticipation of the final coming and total redemption of mankind at the Parousia, God bestowed upon His Son all the supernatural favors that He had prepared for the redeemed human race. These gifts and favors are all contained in the one supreme gift of the Holy Spirit (Acts 2:33).

The clouds which enveloped the Lord (1:9) remind us of the vision of the "Son of Man" of the prophet Daniel (Dan. 7), an apocalyptic figure who will come to judge the world, with whom Jesus identified Himself (Mt. 25:3ff). Thus the angels could proclaim that Christ would return on the last day in the same way as He was taken into heaven.

4. MEDITATION

For many people, the Feast of the Ascension is an anticlimax. The great drama of Good Friday on Calvary and Easter Sunday morning at the empty tomb have raised us to spiritual heights. The next great act in salvation history will be Pentecost, and we have fifty days to get worked up again.

But the feast of the Ascension is one of glorious triumph for Christ. He has fulfilled completely the work the Father had given Him to do, and as a reward for His humble obedience He now enters into glory. This feast, this mystery, consummates the earthly life of Jesus.

Abbot Marmion points out that "in a certain sense, the Ascension is the greatest [feastday] because it is the supreme glorification of Christ Jesus." There is a sense of the magnificent in the liturgical celebration of the feast.

Because Christ worked out His Father's will in and through His human nature, it is only fitting and proper that He would be glorified in His body. It is the logic demanded by congruity that St. Thomas Aquinas and the scholastics so liked.

The feast also includes the notion of Christ, the great and eternal High Priest entering into the Holy of Holies to remain there, eternally, as our one and only Mediator with the Father. This is why we can approach the Throne of God with confidence.

We have seen that the Passion and Death of Christ without the Resurrection is stark and senseless tragedy. It has no meaning. Without the Ascension, the Resurrection would remain an unfinished page in the life and work of Christ.

With Christ, we, His mystical Body, have already entered heaven. It is a pledge of the future glory which we will share individually. Looked at this way, the Feast of the Ascension is not only an opportunity to praise God for the work of His Incarnate Son, it becomes a feast day with huge personal significance.

Far from being an anticlimax, the Ascension is another high point in the work of our salvation, a continuing influence on our own spirituality.

* * * * * * ○ * * * * * * ○ * * * * * *

XIII.
Third Glorious Mystery:
THE DESCENT OF THE HOLY SPIRIT

1. SCRIPTURE

When the day of Pentecost came it found them gathered in one place. Suddenly from up in the sky there came forth a noise like a strong, driving wind which was heard all through the house where they were seated. Tongues as of fire appeared, which parted and came to rest on each of them. All were filled with the Holy Spirit. They began to express themselves in foreign tongues and make bold proclamations as the Spirit prompted them.

Staying in Jerusalem at the time were devout Jews of every nation under heaven. These heard the sound, and assembled in a large crowd. They were much confused because each one heard these men speaking his own language. The whole occurrence astonished them. They asked in utter amazement, "Are not all of these men who are speaking Galileans? How is it that each of us hears them in his native tongue? We are Parthians, Medes and Elamites. We live in Mesopotamia, Judea and Cappadocia, Pontus, the province of Asia, Phrygia and Pamphylia, Egypt and the

regions of Libya around Cyrene. There are even visitors
from Rome — all Jews, or those who have come over to
Judaism; Cretans and Arabs, too. Yet each of us hears them
speaking in his own tongue about the marvels God has
accomplished."

They were dumbfounded, and could make nothing at
all of what had happened. "What does this mean?" they
asked one another, while a few remarked with a sneer,
"They have had too much new wine!"

Peter stood up with the Eleven, raised his voice and
addressed them:

"You who are Jews, indeed all of you staying in
Jerusalem! Listen to what I have to say. You must realize
that these men are not drunk, as you seem to think. It is only
nine in the morning! It is what Joel the prophet spoke of:

> 'It shall come to pass in the last days, says God,
> that I will pour out a portion of my spirit
>   on all mankind:
> Your sons and daughters shall prophesy,
> your young men shall see visions
> And your old men shall dream dreams.
> Yes, even on my servants and handmaids I will pour
>   out a portion of my spirit in those days,
> and they shall prophesy.
> I will work wonders in the heavens above and signs
>   on the earth below:
> blood, fire, and a cloud of smoke.
> The sun shall be turned to darkness and the
>   moon to blood
> before the coming of that great and glorious day
>   of the Lord.
> Then shall everyone be saved who calls on the
>   name of the Lord.'   [Joel 3:1-5]

"Men of Israel, listen to me! Jesus the Nazorean was a man whom God sent to you with miracles, wonders and signs as his credentials. These God worked through him in your midst as you well know. He was delivered up by the set purpose and plan of God; you even made use of pagans to crucify and kill him.

"God freed him from death's bitter pangs, however, and raised him up again, for it was impossible that death should keep its hold on him. David says of him:

'I have set the Lord ever before me,
    with him at my right hand I shall not be
        disturbed.
My heart has been glad and my tongue has rejoiced,
    my body will live on in hope,
for you will not abandon my soul to the nether
        world,
    nor will you suffer your faithful one to undergo
        corruption.
You have shown me the path of life;
    you will fill me with joy in your presence.'

[Psalm 16:8-11]

"Brothers, I can speak confidently to you about our father David. He died and was buried, and his grave is in our midst to this day. He was a prophet and knew that God had sworn to him that one of his descendants would sit upon his throne.

"He said that he was not abandoned to the nether world, nor did his body undergo corruption, thus proclaiming beforehand the resurrection of the Messiah. This is the Jesus God has raised up, and we are his witnesses. Exalted at God's right hand, he first received the promised Holy Spirit from his Father, then poured this Spirit out on us. This is what you now see and hear.

"David did not go up to heaven, yet David says,

'The Lord said to my Lord,
Sit at my right hand
until I make your enemies your footstool.'
[Psalm 110:1]

Therefore let the whole house of Israel know beyond any doubt that God has made both Lord and Messiah this Jesus whom you crucified."

When they heard this they were deeply shaken. They asked Peter and the other apostles, "What are we to do, brothers?"

Peter answered: "You must reform and be baptized, each one of you, in the name of the Lord Jesus Christ, that your sins may be forgiven; then you will receive the gift of the Holy Spirit. It was to you and your children that the promise was made, and to all those still far off whom the Lord our God calls."

In support of his testimony he used many other arguments, and kept urging, "Save yourselves from this generation which has gone astray." Those who accepted his message were baptized; some three thousand were added that day.   Acts 2:1-41   (NAB)

While Apollos was in Corinth, Paul passed through the interior of the country and came to Ephesus. There he found some disciples to whom he put the question, "Did you receive the Holy Spirit when you became believers?" They answered, "We have not so much as heard that there is a Holy Spirit," "Well, how were you baptized?" he persisted. They replied, "With the baptism of John."

Paul then explained, "John's baptism was a baptism of repentance. He used to tell the people about the one who would come after him in whom they were to believe — that is, Jesus." When they heard this, they were baptized in the name of the Lord Jesus. As Paul laid hands on them, the Holy Spirit came down on them and they began to speak in tongues and to utter prophecies. There were in the company about twelve men in all.   Acts 19:1-7   (NAB)

Love never fails. Prophecies will cease, tongues will be silent, knowledge will pass away. . . . There are in the end three things that last: faith, hope and love, and the greatest of these is love.   1 Corinthians 13:8, 13   (NAB)

2. ANCIENT AUTHORS

St. Irenaeus: *Against Heresies*

When the Lord told his disciples "to go and teach all nations, and to baptize them in the name of the Father and of the Son and of the Holy Spirit," he conferred on them the power of giving men new life in God.

He had promised through the prophets that in these last days he would pour out his Spirit on his servants and handmaidens, and that they would prophesy. So when the Son of God became the Son of Man, the Spirit also descended upon him, becoming accustomed in this way to dwelling with the human race, to living in men and to inhabiting God's creation. The Spirit accomplished the Father's will in men who had grown old in sin, and gave them new life in Christ.

Luke says that the Spirit came down on the disciples at Pentecost, after the Lord's ascension, with power to open the gates of life to all nations and to make known to them the new covenant. So it was that men of every language joined in singing one song of praise to God, and scattered tribes, restored to unity by the Spirit, were offered to the Father as the firstfruits of all the nations.

This was why the Lord had promised to send us the Advocate: he was to prepare us as an offering to God. Like dry flour, which cannot become one lump of dough, one loaf of bread, without moisture, we who are many could not become one in Jesus Christ without the water that comes down from heaven.

And like parched ground which yields no harvest unless it receives moisture, we who were once like a waterless tree could never have lived and borne fruit without this abundant rainfall from above. Through the baptism which liberates us from change and decay, we have become one in body; through the Spirit we have become one in soul.

"The Spirit of wisdom and understanding, the Spirit of counsel and strength, the Spirit of knowledge and the fear of God" came down upon the Lord, and the Lord in turn gave this Spirit to the Church, sending the Advocate from heaven into the whole world, into which, according to his own words, the devil, too, had been cast down like lightning.

St. Augustine: *The Trinity*

When He had risen from the dead and appeared to His disciples, He breathed upon them and said, "Receive the Holy Spirit" [Jn 20:20], in order to show that He also proceeded from Himself. And this is the power "which went forth from Him and healed all" [Lk 6:19], as we read in the Gospel.

But as for the reason why He first gave the Holy Spirit on earth after His Resurrection, and later sent Him from heaven, it is, I think, because charity is poured forth in our hearts through Our Lord Himself, by which we love both God and neighbor, according to the two commandments upon which the whole Law and prophets depend [Mt 22:40]

To signify this the Lord twice gave the Holy Spirit, once on earth on account of the love of our neighbor, and again from Heaven on account of the love of God. The Holy Spirit was given when He breathed on them and said, "Go, baptize all nations in the name of the Father and of the Son and of the Holy Spirit" [Mt 28:19], and the same Spirit was given at Pentecost, ten days after the Lord ascended into Heaven.

How great a God is He who gives God!

Blessed Rabanus Maurus: *Veni, Creator Spiritus*

> Come, Holy Spirit, Creator, come
> From your bright heavenly home,
> Come, take possession of our souls
> And make them all your own.
>
> You who are called the Paraclete,
> Best gift of God above,
> The living spring, the living fire,
> Sweet unction and true love.
>
> You who are sevenfold in your grace,
> Finger of God's right hand;
> His promise, teaching little ones
> To speak and understand.
>
> O guide our minds with your blest light,
> With love our hearts inflame;
> And with your strength which ne'er decays,
> Confirm our mortal frame.

Far from us drive our deadly foe;
True peace among us bring;
And from all perils lead us safe
Beneath your sacred wing.

Through you may we the Father know,
Through you the eternal Son,
And you the Spirit of them both,
Thrice-blessed Three in One.

All glory to the Father be,
With his co-equal Son:
The same to you, great Paraclete,
While endless ages run.

3. RECENT AUTHORS

Abbot Columba Marmion: *Fire of Love*

We know indeed how magnificently Jesus fulfilled His divine promise; how ten days after the Ascension, the Holy Spirit, sent by the Father and the Son, descended upon the apostles assembled in the Cenacle, with what abundance of graces and charismata, this Spirit of truth and love was poured forth in the souls of the disciples.

What indeed was the work of the Holy Spirit in the souls of the apostles on the day of Pentecost?

To understand it well, I ought first to recall to you the Church's teaching upon the character of divine works. You know that in the domain of the supernatural life of grace, as well as in the works of natural creation, all that God produces outside Himself, in time, is accomplished by the Father, the Son and the Holy Spirit, without distinction of Persons. The three Persons then act in the unity of their divine nature. The distinction of Persons exists only in the incomprehensible communications that constitute the innermost life of God in Himself.

But in order to remind ourselves more easily of these revelations concerning the divine Persons, the Church, in her language, attributes specially such or such action in one of the three Persons, on account of the affinity that exists between this action and the exclusive properties whereby this Person is distinguished from the others.

Thus the Father is the first principle, proceeding from none other, but from whom proceed the Son and the Holy Spirit. Therefore the work that marks the origin of everything, the creation is especially attributed to Him. Did the Father create alone? Certainly not. The Son and the Holy Spirit created at the same time as the Father, and in union with Him. But between the property, peculiar to the Father, of being the first principle in the divine communications and the work of creation, there is an affinity, in virtue of which the Church can, without error of doctrine, attribute the creation to the Father.

The Son, the Word, is the infinite expression of the thought of the Father. He is considered especially as Wisdom. The works in which this perfection shines forth above all, as in that of ordering the world, are particularly attributed to Him. He is indeed that Wisdom which comes forth out of the mouth of the Most High "reaching from end to end mightily and ordering all things sweetly" (Ant. Dec. 17).

The Church applies the same law to the Holy Spirit. What is He in the adorable Trinity? He is the ultimate term, the consummation of life in God. He closes the intimate cycle of the admirable operations of the divine Life. And this is why, in order that we may remember this property which is personal to Him, the Church specially attributes to Him all that concerns the work of grace, of sanctification, all that concerns the completion, the crowning point, the consummation: He is the divine Artist who, by His least touches, brings the work to its sovereign perfection. The work attributed to the Holy Spirit, in the Church as in souls, is to lead to its end, to its term, to its ultimate perfection, the incessant labor of holiness.

The Holy Spirit, then will fill the apostles with truth, become their spiritual Master, and come to their defense. He will inspire their preaching and fill them with life.

In descending upon them, the Holy Spirit pours forth in them His love, which is Himself. It was necessary that the apostles should be filled with love in order that in preachings the name of Jesus they should give birth to the love of their Master in the souls of those who heard them. It was necessary that their testimony, dictated by the Spirit, should be so full of life as to attach the world to Jesus Christ.

Bishop Charles Francis Buddy: *Going Therefore, Teach*

The Holy Spirit vitalizes the Church, renewing, inspiring and directing her. The Holy Spirit perfects the body of Christ in the life of the Church, enabling her to meet the needs of each age.

The mission of the Third Person of the Blessed Trinity crystallizes the truths taught by Christ. The Holy Spirit forms Christ in the individual to think with the Church, to work zealously for her expansion, to be a torchlight of truth and a messenger of love.

Father Thomas Merton, O.C.S.O.: *Conjectures of a Guilty Bystander*

Since I am a Catholic, I believe, of course, that my Church guarantees for me the highest spiritual freedom. I would not be a Catholic if I did not believe this. I would not be a Catholic if the Church were merely an organization, a collective institution with rules and laws demanding external conformity from its members.

I see the laws of the Church, and all the various ways in which she exercises her teaching authority and her jurisdiction, as subordinate to the Holy Spirit and the law of love. . . . It is in Christ and in His Spirit that true freedom is found, and the Church is His Body, living by His Spirit.

4. MEDITATION

To build up the Body of Christ, which is His Church! That is the work attributed to the Holy Spirit as the legacy of Pentecost. So deep is the mystery considered in the Third Glorious Mystery, so powerful, that no meditation will ever be complete. This mission of the Holy Spirit goes on to the end of time.

However, that does not excuse us from pondering what we do know. The signs and wonders of the original Pentecost Sunday when the Holy Spirit descended on the disciples were also symbols to nourish our faith.

The sound of the wind, a mysterious power to the ancients, speaks of the power of God in the Holy Spirit, because He is God. "Tongues as of fire" remind us of the teaching voice of the Church and the dynamic magisterium *of that Church; the fire — what else could it be but the fire of divine love to which we are called?*

St. Peter's discourse demonstrates how the message of Christ was delivered first to the Jews — it was their promise fulfilled — and then to the Gentiles, those who live afar off, who were included in the mysterious plan of salvation.

The signs and wonders that accompanied the preaching of the first Christians were to attract attention to their message. All too soon the signs became an end in themselves to some who believed. Look at how they tempted Simon Magus (Acts 8:9-24).

So, St. Paul's famous passages in 1 Corinthians, chs. 12-14 were an exhortation to seek the spiritual gifts, but above all, charity, "the more excellent way" which surpasses all the others. We still see some moderns, especially fundamentalists, pursuing the extraordinary gifts as if they were an end in themselves.

The power of the Holy Spirit is alive and well in the Church and we have the divine assurance that it will be, until the consummation of the world.

XIV.

Fourth Glorious Mystery
THE ASSUMPTION

1. SCRIPTURE

I am a flower of Sharon, a lily of the valley.
As a lily among thorns, so is my beloved among women.
As an apple tree among the trees of the wood
    so is my lover among men.
I delight to rest in his shadow,
    and his fruit is sweet to my mouth.
He brings me into the banquet hall
    and his emblem over me is love.
Strengthen me with raisin cakes,
    refresh me with apples,
        for I am faint with love.
His left hand is under my head
    and his right arm embraces me.
I adjure you, daughters of Jerusalem,
    by the gazelles and hinds of the field,
Do not arouse, do not stir up love
    before its own time.
Hark! my lover — here he comes
    springing across the mountains, leaping across
        the hills.

175

My lover is like a gazelle
    or a young stag.
Here he stands behind our wall, gazing through
       the windows,
    peering through the lattices.
My lover speaks; he says to me,
    "Arise, my beloved, my beautiful one,
    and come!"   Song of Songs 2:1-10   (NAB)

With myrrh and aloes and cassia your robes are
      fragrant;
    from ivory palaces string music brings you joy.
The daughters of kings come to meet you;
    the queen takes her place at your right hand in
      gold of Ophir.
Hear, O daughter, and see; turn your ear,
    forget your people and your father's house.
So shall the king desire your beauty;
    for he is your lord, and you must worship him.
And the city of Tyre is here with gifts;
    the rich among the people seek your favor.
All glorious is the king's daughter as she enters;
    her raiment is threaded with spun gold.
In embroidered apparel she is borne in to the king;
    behind her the virgins of her train are brought
      to you.
They are borne in with gladness and joy;
    they enter the palace of the king.
The place of your fathers your sons shall have;
    you shall make them princes through all the land.
I will make your name memorable through all
      generations;
    therefore shall nations praise you forever and ever.
                   Psalm 45:9-18   (NAB)

Blessed are you, daughter, by the Most High God, above all the women on earth; and blessed be the Lord God, the creator of heaven and earth, who guided your blow at the head of the chief of our enemies. Your deed of hope will never be forgotten by those who tell of the might of God. May God make this redound to your everlasting honor, rewarding you with blessings, because you risked your life when your people were being oppressed, and you averted our disaster, walking uprightly before our God.

Judith 13:18-20   (NAB)

2. ANCIENT AUTHORS

St. John Damascene: *Second Sermon on the "Sleep" of the Blessed Virgin Mary*

Today that sacred and living Ark of the living God, in whose womb was conceived the Creator, rests in the temple of the Lord, a temple not built by hands. David, her father, leaps for joy, and even the angels join him in exultation.

On this feast day the Archangels celebrate, the Virtues glorify God, the Principalities exult and are joined in praise by the Powers. The Dominations rejoice and the Thrones cannot restrain their happiness. Cherubim and Seraphim proclaim her glory.

Today, the Eden of the new Adam receives that living Paradise in which the condemnation of old was dissolved, in whom was planted the Tree of Life, through whom our nakedness was covered.

Today the Immaculate Virgin, in whom there is no spot of earthly taint, but only the love of heavenly delights, today she returns not to dust but she is brought into the mansions of Heaven — she, herself, a living Heaven! From her the source of all life was given to mankind. How then could she ever taste death?

She yielded to that law decreed by Him whom she had borne. As a daughter of Adam she submitted to that ancient law, for her Son, Who is Life itself, had not refused it. However, as the Mother of the Living God she was rightfully brought up to Him.

Eve, who had assented to the seduction of the serpent, was condemned to the pains of childbirth and the sentence of death, as well as being detained below. But this blessed woman had listened to the Word of God, had been filled with the Holy Spirit, had agreed to the message of the archangel, and had brought forth the Son of God without sensual pleasure or male seed.

She was totally consecrated to God. How could she possibly feel the pains of childbirth, or know death and corruption, or be detained below? In her body she had carried Life. How definite, how direct, how certain her way to Heaven! "Where I am," says the Life and the Truth, "there shall my servant be." How much more so, then, that His Mother should be joined to Him.

3. RECENT AUTHORS

St. Peter Canisius: *Homily on Mary, the Virgin Mother of God*

The Church joyfully celebrates the feasts of the Mother of God. Spaced throughout the year, they call the faithful to a work eminently worthy of a Christian: honoring that most Blessed Woman, the Mother of Our Lord and God.

Among all the feasts that have been celebrated through the centuries, the Feast of the Assumption is one of the greatest. No other day ever contained such joy and happiness for her, a happiness of both body and soul worthy of our contemplation.

As it had happened before, certainly on this day her body and soul exulted in the Lord, and she could repeat rightfully, "He has regarded the humility of His handmaiden. Behold, from this time on, all generations shall call me blessed. He Who is mighty has done great things to me."

We who love you and your Son, join in praising the wonderful things God has done in you, O truly Blessed Mother, thrice-blessed in the beautiful conclusion by which God has perfected and completed your earthly life.

Blessed, indeed, not only because you have believed, but because you brought forth fruit worthy of that belief. This day you have merited to rejoin Him whom you loved and served with such joy.

Emmanuel entered this world as a stranger, but you received Him into your world as into a palatial manor. Today, you are received by Him into the regal palace of Heaven, to have Him bestow on you the place of honor worthy of the Mother of such a Solomon.

Happy the day on which so precious a treasure is transferred from the desert of this world to the joy of the eternal city. All the blessed of Heaven rejoice on this exceedingly joyful day.

Happy the day on which the gentle, loving Bride finds that which her soul seeks, receives that which she has prayed for, takes possession finally of all that she has hoped for — the eternal vision of God.

Francis Suarez: *Treatise on the Angels*

Certainly even the highest angels welcomed Christ on the Day of the Ascension, as they probably did on the Day of His Resurrection as well.

We can believe the same about the Blessed Virgin on the Day of her Assumption. If it is true (as is piously believed and as the Fathers themselves thought) that Christ Himself came down and assisted in the heavenly ascent of His Mother, certainly the angels did. I hold it for certain that the angels did assist on these occasions, sent by the command and the will of God.

St. Alphonsus Liguori: *The Glories of Mary*

Death being the punishment of sin, it would seem that the divine Mother — all holy, and exempt as she was from its slightest stain — should also have been exempt from death, and from encountering the misfortunes to which the children of Adam, infected by the poison of sin, are subject.

But God was pleased that Mary should in all things resemble Jesus; and as the Son died, it was becoming that the Mother should also die; because, moreover he wished to give the just example of the precious death prepared for them, he willed that even the most Blessed Virgin should die, but by a sweet and happy death.

Let us consider how precious was Mary's death: first on account of the special favors by which it was accomplished; secondly on account of the manner in which it took place.

There are three things that render death bitter: attachment to the world, remorse for sins, and the uncertainty of salvation. The death of Mary was entirely free from these causes of bitterness, and was accompanied by three special graces: she died as she had lived, entirely detached from the things of the world; she died in the most perfect peace; she died in the certainty of eternal glory.

Mary, then, has left the world; she is now in heaven. From there this compassionate Mother looks down on her children in this valley of tears, to comfort and console them, to help them if they wish.

Pope Pius XII: Apostolic Constitution — *Munificentissimus Deus*, Nov. 1950

The Immaculate Mother of God, the ever-Virgin Mary, having completed the course of her earthly life, was assumed body and soul into heavenly glory.

J.W. Langlinais: *The Assumption of Mary*

Pope Pius XII, on Nov. 1, 1950 most solemnly described the crowning event of the life of the Blessed Virgin. Thus defining the dogma of Mary's Assumption, he wrote the final chapter of the centuries long tradition of belief in this mystery.

St. Paul assures the Romans (6:4-13) that through Baptism they are joined to Christ and share in His victory over sin. Mary's unique similarity to Christ began with her conception. Since it is sin and its consequent punishment in death and corruption that delay the final triumph of the ordinary Christian, it is implicit that anyone perfectly free from sin, like Christ, would be free from the deferment of the resurrection of the body. Mary is, also, surely an exception to the rule.

But the most pregnant idea, implied in Scripture and specific already in patristic writings, for accepting and understanding something of the mystery of the Assumption, is that Mary is the New Eve. Three times the Holy Father alludes to the telling comparison, accepting it as an obvious deduction from Scripture and a logical development of Tradition.

Pius XII repeatedly refers to Mary's being the Mother of God as the theological reason for Christ's unique love for

and union with Mary, and for the Assumption. Mary was
united to all three Persons of the Blessed Trinity in a unique
relationship — as privileged daughter, mother and spouse,
privileges that involved her body and soul, that implicated
her in extraordinary sufferings and joys.

Note that the Pope declines to say whether Mary died.
In his defining statement he uses the term, "having completed her earthly life," which offers support neither to the
mortalists (she did die) or the immortalists (she did not die).

The earliest patristic writers simply accept the fact that
she died, and most modern writers do, too. However, it is a
source of controversy among the theologians.

4. MEDITATION

*The controversy about the doctrine of the Assumption, very
alive during my seminary days, always left me wondering why it was
such a big deal. We were taught to believe it as soon as we were old
enough to spell the word for the Sisters.*

*And it seemed so logical. Since Christ had ascended into
heaven, of course He would take His Mother there, as soon as
feasible. That still seems like compelling logic to me.*

*What is the alternative? Well, she died and was buried. But
then a larger question comes up, and a real one. Where? Ephesus
(where it is presumed she lived many of her last days) and Jerusalem
(which seems to have a better claim) both, I am told, have tombs of the
Blessed Mother, but neither one has ever claimed to have her body,
her relics.*

*Those relics would have been a prize treasure. If the bones of
Sts. Peter and Paul are among the top trophies of Rome, what city
would not like to claim Mary's?*

*Pope Pius XII removed this question from the realm of debate
by his definition, and has allowed the theologians free dispute over*

whether or not she actually died as a precondition to her entrance, body and soul, into heaven. I would like to believe that she did not have to die, but the wisdom of the Fathers and the theologians leaves me in a distinct minority.

How much we should rejoice in this mystery of the Rosary! We would need the pen of a St. Bernard or the words of an Archbishop Sheen even to try to imagine the scene in heaven when Mary arrived. What joy, what exultation in the Kingdom of Heaven!

* * * * * * * ◦ * * * * * * * ◦ * * * * * * *

XV.

Fifth Glorious Mystery
THE CORONATION OF OUR LADY

1. SCRIPTURE

One alone is my dove, my perfect one,
    her mother's chosen,
    the dear one of her parent.
The daughters saw her and declared her fortunate,
    the queens and concubines, and they sang
       her praises;
Who is this that comes forth like the dawn,
    as beautiful as the moon, as resplendent as the sun,
    as awe-inspiring as bannered troops?
               Song of Songs 6:9-10D   (NAB)

In the highest heavens did I dwell,
    my throne on a pillar of cloud . . .
    and through all ages I shall not cease to be. . . .
I bud forth delights like the vine,
    my blossoms become fruit fair and rich.
Come to me, all you that yearn for me,
    and be filled with my fruits;
               Sirach 24:4, 9b, 17-18   (NAB)

187

When one finds a worthy wife,
    her value is far beyond pearls.
Her husband, entrusting his heart to her,
    has an unfailing prize.
She brings him good and not evil,
    all the days of her life.
She obtains wool and flax
    and makes cloth with skillful hands.
Like merchant ships,
    she secures her provisions from afar.
She rises while it is still night,
    and distributes food to her household.
She picks out a field to purchase;
    out of her earning she plants a vineyard.
She is girt about with strength,
    and sturdy are her arms.
She enjoys the success of her dealings;
    at night her lamp is undimmed.
She puts her hands to the distaff,
    and her fingers ply the spindle.   .
She reaches out her hands to the poor,
    and extends her arms to the needy.
She fears not the snow for her household;
    all her charges are doubly clothed.
She makes her own coverlets;
    fine linen and purple are her clothing.
Her husband is prominent at the city gates
    and he sits with the elders of the land.
She makes garments and sells them,
    and stocks the merchants with belts.
She is clothed with strength and dignity,
    and she laughs at the days to come.
She opens her mouth in wisdom,
    and on her tongue is kindly counsel.

She watches the conduct of her household,
    and she eats not her food in idleness.
Her children rise up and praise her;
    her husband, too, extols her:
    "Many are the women of proven worth,
    but you have excelled them all."
Charm is deceptive and beauty fleeting;
    the woman who fears the Lord is to be praised.
Give her a reward of her labors,
    and let her works praise her at the city gates.
Proverbs 31:10-31   (NAB)

A great sign appeared in the sky, a woman clothed with the sun, with the moon under her feet, and on her head a crown of twelve stars. Because she was with child, she wailed aloud in pain as she labored to give birth.
Revelation 12:1-2   (NAB)

2. ANCIENT AUTHORS

St. Bonaventure: *On the Regal Dignity of the Blessed Virgin Mary*

The Blessed Virgin Mary is the Mother of the Most High King, conceived in loving acceptance according to the angelic message, "Behold, you will conceive and bear a Son."

Take this in conjunction with the other verse, "The Lord will give Him the throne of David, His Father. He will rule over the House of Jacob forever and His reign will never end." It is as if the angel plainly stated, "You will conceive and bear a King for a Son, Who will rule in eternal splendor. Through Him, you, the Mother of the King, will reign as a Queen, co-ruler in His eternal splendor."

If it is necessary for a son to honor his mother, then certainly a King must share the royal dignity with his mother. The Virgin Mother has conceived and brought forth Him Who has emblazoned before Him, "King of Kings and Lord of Lords!"

From the instant she conceived the Son of God, she became the Queen of Heaven and earth. This designation is revealed in the Apocalypse by the words, "A great sign has appeared in the heavens, a woman clothed with the sun, with the moon under her feet, and on her head a crown of twelve stars."

That Mary is Queen and outstanding in her glory, is chanted by the Psalmist in that psalm especially prophetical of Christ and His Virgin Mother, "Your throne, O God, exists forever." Then he adds of Our Lady, "The Queen shall sit at Your right side." This indicates her outstanding power.

He follows with the words, "Robed in gold," to express the glorious gift of corporal immortality shown by her Assumption. Never could it happen that the body which enveloped the Word-made-flesh, which was perfectly sanctified on earth, could ever return to dust, to be the food of worms.

Mary the Queen dispenses grace, as is intimated in the book of Esther, "A little fountain pouring forth a whole torrent is turned into laughing rivulets of sunlight." The Virgin Mary is compared to Esther as to a fountain with a two-fold use. She pours forth the light and the grace of both action and contemplation.

The grace of God, so necessary to heal mankind, is dispensed to us through her. As from an aqueduct, grace flows through Mary. What her Son won by strict right, Mary dispenses as a most merciful Queen, compassionating her needy people.

Hermanus Contractus: *Salve Regina*

Hail, Holy Queen, mother of mercy,
our life, our sweetness and our hope.
To you do we cry, poor banished children of Eve.
To you do we send up our sighs,
mourning and weeping in this vale of tears.
Turn then, most gracious advocate,
your eyes of mercy toward us, and,
after this, our exile
show us the fruit of your womb: Jesus.

O clement, O loving, O sweet Virgin Mary! *
                    (* probably added by St. Bernard)

3. RECENT AUTHORS

St. Peter Canisius: *Homily on Mary,
the Virgin Mother of God*

Why did the Fathers of the Church call the Virgin Mary by the title "Queen"? They recognized the tremendous praise heaped on her in the Scriptures. She is singled out as having a King for her father, noble David, and the King of Kings and Lord of Lords as her Son, whose reign shall never end.

There is not one who excels her in dignity, beauty or holiness. Only the Holy Trinity is above her; all others are below her in dignity and beauty.

Happy the day on which the most humble of hand-maidens is raised to her position as Queen of Heaven and most powerful Mistress of the world. No higher position is possible in her Son's Kingdom. Her throne is right next to Christ's in glory.

Happy and venerable is the day on which this Queen and Mother is given so powerful and merciful a position that she will be our merciful protectress at the throne of the Divine Judge, her Son.

Cardinal John Henry Newman: *On the Fitness of the Glories of Mary*

The king asked, "What should be done to the man whom the king desires to honor?" and he received the following answer, "The man whom the king wishes to honor ought to be clad in the king's apparel, and to be mounted on the king's saddle, and to receive the royal diadem on his head; and let the first among the princes and presidents hold his horse and let them walk before him through the streets of the city, and say, 'Thus shall be honored whom the king has a mind to honor.' "

So stands the case with Mary; she gave birth to the Creator, and what recompense shall be made her? What shall be done to her, who had this relationship to the Most High? What shall be the fit accompaniment of one whom the Almighty has deigned to make, not His servant, not His friend, not His intimate, but His superior, the source of His second being, the nurse of His helpless infancy, the teacher of His opening years?

I answer as the king was answered: Nothing is too high for her to whom God owes His human life; no exuberance of grace, no excess of glory, but is becoming, but is to be expected there, where God has lodged Himself, whence God has issued.

Let her "be clad in the king's apparel," that is, let the fullness of the Godhead so flow into her that she may be the figure of the incommunicable sanctity, and beauty, and glory, of God Himself: that she be the Mirror of Justice, the

Mystical Rose, the Tower of Ivory, the House of Gold, the Morning Star.

Let her "receive the king's diadem upon her head," as the Queen of heaven, the Mother of all living, the Health of the weak, the Refuge of sinners, the Comforter of the afflicted. And "let the first among the king's princes walk before her," let angels and prophets and apostles and martyrs and all saints kiss the hem of her garment.

Pope Pius XII: *Ad Caeli Reginam* (Queenship of Mary) Oct. 11, 1954

1.   From the earliest ages of the Catholic Church a Christian people, whether in time of triumph or more especially in time of crisis, has addressed prayers of petition and hymns of praise and veneration to the Queen of Heaven. And never has that hope wavered which they placed in the Mother of the Divine King, Jesus Christ; nor has that faith ever failed by which we are taught that Mary, the Virgin Mother of God, reigns with a mother's solicitude over the entire world, just as she is crowned in heavenly blessedness with the glory of a Queen.

5.   And now, that we may bring the year of Mary to a happy and beneficial conclusion, and in response to petitions which have come to us from around the world, We have decided to institute the liturgical feast of the Blessed Virgin Mary, Queen. This will afford a climax, as it were, to the manifold demonstrations of our devotion to Mary, which the Christian people have supported with such enthusiasm.

6.   In this matter we do not wish to propose a new truth to be believed by Christians, since the title and the arguments on which Mary's queenly dignity are based have

already been clearly set forth and are to be found in ancient documents of the Church and in the books of the sacred liturgy.

34.   According to ancient traditions and the sacred liturgy the main principle on which the royal dignity of Mary rests is without doubt her divine Motherhood. So with complete justice, St. John Damascene could write, "When she became the mother of the Creator, she truly became the Queen of every creature." Likewise it can be said that the heavenly voice of the archangel Gabriel was the first to proclaim Mary's royal office.

Francis Suarez: *Treatise on the Angels*

With regard to the most excellent Virgin Mary, as the Church herself sings, she is exalted above all the choirs of angels in the heavenly kingdom. It is certain that among all creatures, no matter how pure, the Blessed Virgin exceeds all in beatitude, even the angels.

Furthermore, it is exceedingly probable that even though she alone is superior to all in essential beatitude, a few of the saints may be equal to the highest orders of angels in perfection. In general, though, we can say that the angels are higher than men.

4. MEDITATION

There are certain titles of the Blessed Mother's that Catholics are a little bit protective of, and even a bit shy of proclaiming at large. That "Mary was crowned Queen of heaven and earth," seems to make this Fifth Glorious Mystery particularly Catholic. Nothing could be further from the truth.

This is a title that Christians have always given to her, going back as far into Christian history as we can. Long before schisms and heresies tore at the "seamless robe of Christ," long before the assault on the Christian unity of the Body of Christ, His Church loved to give this title to Mary.

It is such a logical devotion. Christ the New Adam; Mary the New Eve. Christ the Son; Mary the Mother. Christ the King; Mary the Queen. Liturgical usage, the way the Church prays officially, has encouraged this title. Popular devotion has long since accepted the crowning of statues of Mary.

"To Jesus through Mary" has long been regarded as a safe path to become more Christ-like. True Marian devotion always leads to a greater understanding and appreciation of the divinity of Christ. Like the Rosary itself, Marian devotion has proven itself through time and circumstances.

The power of the mysteries of the Rosary increases with use. It has drawn countless numbers of Christians into the heart of the Incarnation.

* * * * * * * o * * * * * * * o * * * * * * *

Addenda:
ALTERNATIVE MYSTERIES

The fifteen mysteries of the Rosary with which we are most familiar are the customary steps of the rosary devotion. However, for special occasions or for the sake of variety, other topics in the life of Our Lord and Our Lady may be chosen.

Here are a few suggestions, in simple form.

1. THE MARRIAGE FEAST OF CANA

A. *Scripture*

On the third day there was a wedding at Cana in Galilee, and the mother of Jesus was there. Jesus and his disciples had likewise been invited to the celebration. At a certain point the wine ran out, and Jesus' mother told him, "They have no more wine." Jesus replied, "Woman, how does this concern of yours involve me? My hour has not yet come."

His mother instructed those waiting on table, "Do whatever he tells you."

As prescribed for Jewish ceremonial washing, there were at hand six stone water jars, each one holding fifteen to twenty-five gallons. "Fill those jars with water," Jesus ordered, at which they filled them to the brim. "Now," he said, "draw some out and take it to the waiter in charge."

They did as he instructed them. The waiter in charge tasted the water made wine, without knowing where it had come from; only the waiters knew, since they had drawn the water.

Then the waiter in charge called the groom over and remarked to him: "People usually serve the choice wine first; then when the guests have been drinking awhile, a lesser vintage. What you have done is keep the choice wine until now."

Jesus performed this first of his signs at Cana in Galilee. Thus did he reveal his glory, and his disciples believed in him.   John 2:1-12   (NAB)

B. Reading

Father Joseph-Marie Perrin, O.P.: *Mary: Mother of Christ and of Christians*

"They have no wine." Down through the centuries Christian writers have used this theme for meditation and have pondered the richness of its meaning, relating it instinctively to almost basic need: to Charity, that wine which intoxicates the heart.

Nevertheless, this prayer of the Mother of Jesus, despite its perfection, seems to face an impossible situation. It involves something with grave consequences.

His hour had not yet come. Yet, at her request, the hour at which His public life begins has arrived. It is not a question of the passing of time, but of the mysterious cooperation by which God accomplishes his plans.

C. Meditation

Christian spiritual writers see a connection with the sanctity of Christian marriage and the fact that Christ graced a marriage feast with His very first recorded public miracle. It is certainly a blessing that Christ pointed out marriage as a very special state of life.

After all, it is the ordinary route to Heaven. The Church has never canonized anyone simply as "husband" or "wife," "father" or "mother" because it expects that all who live up to the graces of this vocation will certainly arrive in Heaven.

But there are other points to ponder at Cana of Galilee. Why did Mary expect Christ to "do something" for the bride and groom? What did she know that no evangelist has ever recorded? I wouldn't doubt that Christ had already worked miracles for her, privately, unobtrusively and quietly. She certainly knew her Jesus, and the brief exchange between them is a wonder.

Then there is the size of those water jars. Think how much five gallons of water weighs, and these were three to five times as heavy!

And St. John is quite charitable about those first disciples. One little miracle and they believed in Him. What did they believe? Probably this got only enough attention from them to begin to look at Him as a very special teacher or a prophet. It took the Resurrection (and for some, more) to get them to believe in His divinity.

But this passage of St. John's records Mary's last word. "Whatever my Son tells you to do, do." That is Mary's message to us and to the whole world, and it sums up the whole direction of Mariology.

2. THE BEATITUDES

A. *Scripture*

> How blest are the poor in spirit:
>   the reign of God is theirs.
> Blest too are the sorrowing;
>   they shall be consoled.
> Blest are the lowly;
>   they shall inherit the land.
> Blest are they who hunger and thirst for holiness;
>   they shall have their fill.
> Blest are they who show mercy;
>   mercy shall be theirs.
> Blest are the single-hearted;
>   for they shall see God.
> Blest too the peacemakers;
>   they shall be called sons of God.
> Blest are those persecuted for holiness' sake;
>   the reign of God is theirs.
> Blest are you when they insult you and persecute
>   you and utter every kind of slander against you
>   because of me.
> Be glad and rejoice,
>   for your reward is great in heaven;
> They persecuted the prophets before you
>   in the very same way.   Matthew 5:3-12   (NAB)

> Blest are you poor;
>   the reign of God is yours.
> Blest are you who hunger;
>   you shall be filled.
> Blest are you who are weeping;
>   you shall laugh.

Blest shall you be when men hate you, when they ostracize you and insult you and proscribe your name as evil because of the Son of Man. On the day they do so, rejoice and exult, for your reward shall be great in heaven. Thus it was that their fathers treated the prophets.

Luke 6:20-23   (NAB)

B. Reading

John L. McKenzie: *Dictionary of the Bible*

(The beatitudes are built on paradox.) The paradox consists in this, that the beatitude is declared not because of some good fortune, but because of ill fortune — poverty, hunger, sorrow and persecution. Jesus states that in these things men may be happy if they accept them as coming from their heavenly Father and in the spirit in which Jesus teaches them.

He thus declares that the opposite of these things — wealth, joy, fullness — have nothing to do with one's true happiness, which is to be found only in the kingdom of God and in His righteousness.

The paradox and the blessedness are extended in Matthew by the addition of some difficult habits of virtue, which demand the suppression of self-love and ambition.

C. Meditation

The Sermon on the Mount has been called the "Charter of the Kingdom" because it points out the ways of Christian living. The negative aspect of death to sin by conversion and baptism must have, then, a positive aspect in the life of baptismal grace and a life of virtue.

Some people seem to think that the early Christians lived in a perpetual state of prayers and praises, sort of a life-time "revival." In the enthusiasm of the first Pentecost, and with the feeling that Christ was about to return in glory momentarily, this may have been the first reaction.

But the first Christians were Jewish people, a race which is practical and down to earth. They had children to feed and homes to tend and work to do. They proceeded through enthusiasm to a type of "communitarianism" where they held all things in common, to a settled Church under a very firm organization: bishop, priests and deacons.

Since the New Testament as we know it was not in circulation until long after the death of St. John, they treasured what they remembered and what was written down locally. Through it all shines the teachings of the Sermon on the Mount.

Blessed are those who are familiar with these teachings.

3. THE CHURCH FOUNDED UPON ST. PETER

A. Scripture

When Jesus came to the neighborhood of Caesarea Philippi, he asked his disciples this question: "Who do people say that the Son of Man is?" They replied, "Some say John the Baptizer, others Elijah, still others Jeremiah or one of the prophets."

"And you," he said to them, "who do you say that I am?"

"You are the Messiah," Simon Peter answered, "the Son of the living God."

Jesus replied, "Blest are you, Simon son of John. No mere man has revealed this to you, but my heavenly Father. I for my part declare to you, you are 'Rock,' and on this rock I will build my Church, and the jaws of death shall not prevail against it.

"I will entrust to you the keys of the kingdom of heaven. Whatever you shall declare bound on earth shall be bound in heaven; whatever you declare loosed on earth shall be loosed in heaven."

Then he strictly ordered his disciples not to tell anyone that he was the Messiah.   Matthew 16:13-20   (NAB)

When they had eaten their meal, Jesus said to Simon Peter, "Simon, son of John, do you love me more than these?" "Yes, Lord," he said, "you know that I love you." At which Jesus said, "Feed my lambs."

A second time he put his question, "Simon, son of John, do you love me?" "Yes, Lord," Peter said, "you know that I love you." Jesus replied, "Tend my sheep."

A third time Jesus asked him, "Simon, son of John, do you love me?" Peter was hurt because he had asked a third time, "Do you love me?" So he said to him: "Lord, you know everything. You know well that I love you." Jesus said to him, "Feed my sheep."   John 21:15-17   (NAB)

B. Reading

Vatican Council I: *Pastor Aeternus*, #4

We teach and define that it is a dogma divinely revealed: that the Roman Pontiff, when he speaks *ex cathedra*, that is, when in the discharge of the office of pastor and doctor of all Christians, by virtue of his supreme apostolic authority, he defines a doctrine regarding faith or morals to be held by the universal Church, by the divine assistance promised him in blessed Peter, is possessed of that infallibility with which the Divine Redeemer willed that His Church should be endowed for defining doctrine regarding faith or morals: and that therefore such definitions of the Roman Pontiff are irreformable of themselves, and not from the consent of the Church.

C. Meditation

The power of infallibility that Christ left with His Church is sometimes difficult for adult converts to comprehend, at first. Yet, if we look at it as Christ conferring on St. Peter and his successors the leadership or government of the Church, and in the act giving him all the executive, legislative and judicial power, it begins to make sense.

Christ did not establish a democratic Church. He gave it a human leader who would remain after the Ascension, in an office that would go on as long as the Church — to the end of time. This leadership is not a lordly one, nor is it meant to be exercised in any way divorced from the basic Christian law of Charity.

It is really a service function, since, should there be great questions that the theologians cannot solve, nor the bishops, then there is always the appeal of last resort, to the Holy Father, the successsor of St. Peter. The Church needs it as the Body of Christ; we need it as members of that Body.

It is the voice of the dynamic **magisterium** *of the Church.*

* * * * * * * o * * * * * * * o * * * * * * *

AUTHOR INDEX

205